The Great Meadows with Fort Necessity outlined in the center—1904

Washington's Expeditions
(1753-1754)
and
Braddock's Expedition
(1755)

with a
History of Tom Fausett
the
Slayer of General Edward Braddock

James Hadden

HERITAGE BOOKS
2006

HERITAGE BOOKS
AN IMPRINT OF HERITAGE BOOKS, INC.

Books, CDs, and more—Worldwide

For our listing of thousands of titles
see our website
at
www.HeritageBooks.com

A Facsimile Reprint
Published 2006 by
HERITAGE BOOKS, INC.
Publishing Division
65 East Main Street
Westminster, Maryland 21157-5026

Copyright © 1910 James Hadden
Entered according to act of congress in the year 1910, by
James Hadden, Uniontown, Pa., in the office of the
Librarian of Congress at Washington, D.C.

Copyright © 2003 Heritage Books, Inc.

— Publisher's Notice —
In reprints such as this, it is often not possible to remove
blemishes from the original. We feel the contents of this
book warrant its reissue despite these blemishes and
hope you will agree and read it with pleasure.

International Standard Book Number:
978-0-7884-2337-1

List of Illustrations

Page.

The Great Meadows with Fort Necessity Outlined in the Center—1904..Frontispiece

Major George Washington—1754........ 8

Rock Fort where the Half-King was Encamped 22

Ledge of Rocks from which Washington Fired on the French 26

Jumonville's Grave 28

Road over which Washington's men pulled the cannon by hand 32

Fort Necessity as sketched by Freeman Lewis—1816 54

Washington's Mill, built in Fayette County—1776 58

List of Illustrations (Continued)

Chapter II.

	Page
General Edward Braddock	66
Fort Cumberland—1755	70
Braddock's Battlefield	80
Dunbar's Encampment	86
Braddock's Watch	98
Braddock's Grave	104

Chapter III.

Washington's Springs	120
Peddler's Rocks	124
Rebecca Fausett, Grand-daughter of Joseph Fausett	130
Grave of Thomas Fausett	138

Preface.

In presenting this narrative of the expeditions of Lieutenant Colonel George Washington and Major General Edward Braddock to the public it is with the belief that a short and comprehensive relation of these two important events in the history of our country will prove both interesting and instructive.

These expeditions were the initiatives of a great struggle between two great powers to decide whether America was to be an appendage of France or to become the land of an English-speaking race.

The great Mississippi valley, a region vast enough and fertile enough to feed the inhabitants of the world, was a goal far more to be desired than for which the armies of the nations had ever before contended.

Not only this, but these expeditions schooled the colonists in the arts of war and gave them that confidence in their prowess that enabled them later successfully to throw off the yoke of oppression and establish a new nation which is now attracting the wonder and admiration of the civilized world.

WASHINGTON'S EXPEDITIONS—
1753-1754.

Washington's Mission to the French Posts at the Head of the Allegheny River, 1753.

More than a century had elapsed after the discovery of this continent by the Cabots before the first English settlement was established in America, and one hundred and forty years more had rolled away before settlements were attempted west of the Allegheny mountains. Thus for two hundred and fifty years after having gained possession by discovery had England been content to colonize only the American seaboard.

The French had made settlements on the St. Lawrence, and by the last half of the seventeenth century had pushed their way along the shore of the great lakes, and by the middle of the eighteenth century had explored the country from the lakes on the north to the gulf on the south and from the Alleghenies on the east to the Mississippi on the west, and had established their trading posts and their missions.

Although a lucrative business had been carried on for some years by Pennsylvania, Maryland and Virginia fur traders with the Indians of the Ohio Valley, no systematic effort on the part of the English colonists had been made to establish settlements west of the Allegheny mountains until 1748, when Thomas Lee, president of the Virginia council, associated with himself twelve other gentlemen, among whom were Gov. Robert Dinwiddie, Lawrence and Augustine Washington — brothers of George Washington, and Mr. John Hamburg, a wealthy merchant of London. This company was to be known as the Ohio Company, and a royal grant was obtained in March, 1749, for a tract of five hundred thousand acres of land lying on the south side of the Ohio and between the Monongahela and the Kanawha rivers, with privilege to embrace a portion of land on the north side if deemed expedient. Two hundred thousand acres were to be selected immediately, the whole to be exempt from quit rent for ten years, the company agreeing

Major George Washington—1754

to seat one hundred families on the same within seven years, and at their own expense to build a fort and maintain a garirison sufficient to protect the settlement.

Christopher Gist was employed as the agent for this Ohio company to select the lands and to conciliate the Indians. With these objects in view he left his home on the banks of the Yodkin, near the boundary line between Virginia and North Carolina, in the fall of 1749, and ascended the Potomac to the mouth of Will's creek. From here, on the thirty-first of October, he proceeded to where Bedford is now located, and from thence to the Forks of the Ohio. At Logstown, about sixteen miles below the Forks, a conference was held with Tanacharisson, a Seneca chief of great note, he being head Sachem of the mixed tribes, which had migrated to the Ohio and its tributaries. He was generally surnamed the Half-King, being subordinate to the Iroquois confederacy, and was a man of considerable intelligence. After the usual formalities and the delivery of many presents in securing the friendship of the Indians, Gist passed on down the Ohio river to within fifteen miles of the falls, and thence by a circuitous route he returned to Virginia in 1751.

In 1750 the Ohio Company built a small storehouse on the site once occupied by the Shawanese town Cainctucuc on the west side of Will's creek where that stream empties into the Potomac river and where the city of Cumberland now stands, and the following year Colonel Thomas Cresap, who then lived at Shawnee Oldtown, was employed to open out a road from Will's creek to the mouth of the Monongahela. He wisely selected for his assistant a Delaware Indian by the name of Nemacolin, whose residence was at the mouth of Nemacolin's creek, now known as Dunlap's creek, on the Monongahela river. Beginning at the terminus of the road already made, to the storehouse at Will's creek, they followed an old trail worn by the foot of the red man centuries before the pale face beheld the outlines of a new continent. Running westward until reaching the crest of Laurel Hill this road turned abruptly northward along the crest of the mountain and descended the western slope, where it joined the old Catawba trail on what is known as the

Mt. Braddock farm. From this point northward this road was, with few deviations, identical with the above mentioned trail, crossing the Youghiogheny river a short distance below the present town of New Haven, passing to the west of the location of Mount Pleasant, and when reaching a point to the west of the location of Greensburg it deflected to the west and on to the Forks of the Ohio. From the fact that Nemacolin was employed on the improvement of the trail it received the name of Nemacolins trail, which name it retained until Braddock's army passed over it, since which it has been known as Braddock's road.

Gist made a second survey for the Ohio Company in 1752, this time passing over the Nemacolin trail and crossing the Monongahela below where McKeesport now stands. Returning, he crossed the Monongahela at the mouth of Nemacolin creek, where he met his old Indian friend, who proposed the following question: "If the French claim all the land north of the Ohio, and the English all on the south, where do the

Indians' lands lie?" This question went unanswered.

Gist had selected for himself twenty-five hundred acres of land at the foot of Laurel Hill, considering this within the Ohio Company's grant, and in 1753 he here established a small settlement consisting of eleven families. He built his cabin near a fine spring and within a few rods of the exact geographical center of Fayette county. He was the second settler within the bounds of what is now Fayette county, Wendell Brown having preceded him by one year.

In 1753 the French began active measures to secure the Ohio valley by the force of arms by erecting a cordon of forts to extend from Lake Erie down the Allegheny and Ohio rivers. This news soon reached the ears of the governor of Virginia, who in the fall of the same year determined to dispatch a messenger to demand of the French an explanation of their design and warn them off.

George Washington, then in his twenty-second year, was commissioned by Governor Dinwiddie as a special envoy to proceed to the headwaters of the Allegheny and deliver the message to Gen-

BRADDOCK'S EXPEDITIONS 13

eral St. Pierre, the French commander. He started out on his journey October thirtieth, the day or the day after he had received his credentials, and arrived at Will's creek November fourteenth. Here he secured the services of Christopher Gist as guide, John Davidson as Indian interpreter, Captain Jacob Van Braam as French interpreter; Curram and McQuire, Indian traders, and Stewart and Jenkins—these four as servitors.

From here they followed the Nemacolin trail, passing Gist's new settlement, and after seven days reached Frazer's trading post at the mouth of Turtle creek, on the Monongahela river. Passing on down they arrived at Logstown, about sixteen miles below the Forks, after sunset November twenty-fourth. Here a consultation was held with Tanacharission, the Half-King; Monacatootha, the next in command, and other friendly Indians of the mixed tribes, some of which Washington engaged to accompany him to Venango, the advance post of the French. Here they arrived December fourth, and found the French flag flying over the log house from which Frazier, the English trader, had been driven and which was now occupied by Joncaire, who referred Washington to the commanding officer, whose headquarters were at La Boeuf, the fort lately built a short distance above on French creek. Here he was courteously received by Legardeur de St. Pierre, who promised to forward his message to the governor-general of Canada, and refused to discuss the great questions involving the remonstrance of Virginia, but stated that he would in the meantime hold his position to the best of his ability, and intended, further, to eject every Englishman from the Ohio valley.

His mission fulfilled, Washington, after much delay, started back, and becoming impatient of the company he and Gist alone concluded to strike out on foot across the country. After much fatigue and suffering, being shot at by a treacherous Indian and nearly lost in the Allegheny river, they reached Frazer's house once more. They left Frazer's on January 1, 1754, and reached Gist's plantation on Jaunary second. Here they procured horses and pressed on, reaching Will's creek on the sixth. Washing-

BRADDOCK'S EXPEDITIONS 15

ton spent the night with Gist, and met seventeen horses loaded with material and stores for the fort at the Forks of the Ohio, and the day after some families going out to settle. The Ohio Company, having determined to build their fort at the Forks and to establish trading posts at Frazer's and elsewhere, were proceeding energetically toward the accomplishment of these objects. He delivered the message of Saint Pierre and made a full report of his journey to the governor at Williamsburg on the sixteenth of January; thus Washington's first important public service was accomplished.

Before Washington had returned from his mission to the French forts the Ohio Company had appealed to Governor Dinwiddie for military protection at their fort already begun at the Forks, in compliance with which, early in January of 1754, Wm. Trent, an explorer, who at this time was engaged in erecting a strong log storehouse at the mouth of Redstone creek on the Monongahela river for the Ohio Company—this being the next storehouse west of that already built at Will's creek, was commissioned as captain, John Frazer, before mentioned, as lieutenant, and Edward Ward, appointed as ensign, were authorized to raise a company of militia of one hundred men, proceed to the Forks and finish and garrison the fort already begun.

Trent proceeded by Nemacolin's trail as far as Gist's plantation, and from thence to the mouth of Redstone, where after finishing the Hangard he returned to Will's creek, leaving Ensign Ward in command to proceed to the Forks, at which place he arrived on the seventeenth of February. Here with Gist and George Croghan they proceeded to finish the fort, which was supplied with ten four-pound field pieces and eighty barrels of powder and a supply of small arms.

The French descend the Allegheny in considerable force.

Everything seemed quiet until the Allegheny, freed from ice, opened in the spring. On April thirteenth Ensign Ward received notice that the French were descending the river in considerable force.

The following day he dispatched a letter to Captain Trent at Will's creek, and went directly himself to Lieutenant Frazer at Turtle creek, who replied that he could not leave his work, as by doing so he would lose shillings for every pence he would receive for his services. The following morning Ensign Ward sent for the Half-King and one of his chiefs named Serreneatta, and set to work to finish the stockade. They had the last gate erected before the French appeared.

On the seventeenth Contrecoeur appeared before the fort with three hundred wooden canoes and sixty bateaux with four men to each, eighteen pieces of cannon, three of which were nine-pounders. A landing was made a small distance from the fort, and Le Mercier was sent to demand a surrender of the fort. Looking at his watch, which indicated two o'clock, he demanded that an answer be delivered at the French camp in writing within one hour. Ensign Ward spent half of this hour in consulting with the Half-King, who advised him to acquaint the French commander that he was not an officer of rank, nor invested with power to answer his demand, and to request him to await the arrival of the principal commander. Contrecoeur was inflexible, and demanded an answer that instant.

Ward saw the French to number about a thousand, and his own force being forty-one in all—only thirty-three of which were soldiers, he surrendered, with liberty to march off with everything belonging thereto by twelve o'clock the next day. He encamped within three hundred yards of the fort with a party of friendly Indians. The French commander sent for him to supper and made many inquiries as to the intention of the English, but Ward refused to impart the desired information. The commander then tried to buy some carpenter tools, which Ward refused to sell.

The following morning Ensign Ward received a speech from Half-King to the governor and proceeded with all his men to Redstone, where he arrived in two days, and from there to Will's creek, where he arrived on the twenty-second and met Colonel Washington on his way to the Forks.

The French immediaely completed

the stockade evacuated by Ensign Ward and named it Fort Duquesne in honor of the governor-general of Canada.

The reply of the French general, Saint Pierre, together with the information received from Washington, convinced Governor Dinwiddie that inaction on his part would lose to the English the whole valley of the Ohio.

Washington is commissioned Major and ordered against the French.

He therefore commissioned Washington as major, with authority to enlist one hundred and fifty men and proceed to the Forks of the Ohio to finish the fort already begun, to make prisoners and to kill or destroy all who interrupted the English settlement. This commission was soon raised to that of lieutenant-colonel, and the number of men increased to three hundred, to be divided into six companies. Enlistments were encouraged by a royal grant of two hundred thousand acres of land, to be divided among them. Colonel Joshua Fry, an English gentleman, was appointed to command the whole, and was to follow with the artillery to be conveyed up the Potomac. The first intention was to make a wagon road from Will's creek, to which point the Ohio Company had already opened a road, to the mouth of Redstone, and there erect a fort; thence, when reenforced, to proceed against the French at the Forks. With these objects in view Washington started from Alexandria, Virginia, April 2, 1754, with two companies, amounting to one hundred and fifty men, and having been joined on the route by a detachment under Captain Adam Stephens, arrived at Will's creek, April twentieth, and two days later Ensign Ward arrived with the intelligence of the surrender of the works at the Fork of the Ohio.

From here sixty men were sent forward to widen the Nemacolin trail, and and April twenty-ninth the army moved from Will's creek, and by the ninth of May were encamped at the Little Meadows, a distance of twenty miles. Here Washington received information that Contrecoeur had been reenforced with eight hundred men, and expresses were immediately sent to the governors of Pennsylvania, Virginia and Maryland requesting reenforcements, and after consultation with his brother officers decided to advance. Casleman creek was two miles west of Little Meadows, and here more than two days were spent in bridging the stream; this was named the Little Crossings. On the eighteenth the Youghiogheny river was reached, seventeen miles west of the Little Crossings, and although the army was enabled to cross without bridging, this place was named the Big Crossings.

While the army lay here several days Washington, with Lieutenant West, three soldiers and an Indian descended the river in a canoe to ascertain if it was navigable for the transportation of the artillery, which they had been obliged to drag by hand since leaving Will's creek. This journey ended in disappointment at the Falls, a distance of thirty miles from the Great Crossings. Scarcely had Washington returned from his journey to the falls when a messenger arrived from his old friend, the Half-King, that a detachment of French were marching toward him with a determination to make an attack, and that he (the Half-King) would be on in five days to hold a council. Washington thereupon hastened to the Great Meadows, a distance of about fifty-one miles west of Will's creek, reaching this place on the twenty-fourth of May, and here he again received intelligence that the French were on their way to meet him. A halt was made and a stockade erected, and by clearing away the brush and undergrowth, prepared, as he said, "a most charming field for an encounter."

A scouting party was sent out on wagon horses to reconnoitre, but returned without having seen an enemy. The same evening the Half-King's warning was confirmed by a trader, who told that the French were at the crossing of the Youghiogheny, eighteen miles distant from the Big Crossings, and known as Stewart's Crossing, as William Stewart lived near that place in 1753 and part of 1754, and was driven out by the French.

About two o'clock in the night an alarm was given. The sentries fired upon what they mistook to be prowling foes; the troops sprang to arms and remained on the alert until daybreak. Not an enemy was to be seen. The roll was

Rock Fort where the Half-King was encamped

called and six men were missing, having deserted.

On May twenty-seventh Mr. Gist came in and reported that La Force, with a detachment of about fifty men, had been seen at his place, about fifteen miles distant, and that he had just come upon their tracks within five miles of the camp, whereupon Washington sent a detachment of seventy-five men in pursuit of him and his band, but the scouts returned without having discovered the enemy.

The Half-King Joins Washington.

Between eight and nine o'clock that same night a messenger arrived from Half-King, who with his followers was then encamped at the Big Rock, about six miles off, with the information that he had tracked two men who were out as scouts, and was satisfied that the whole force was in ambush near by. Washington, fearing a stratagem, left a strong guard to protect the baggage, and with a detachment of forty men set out before ten o'clock to join the Indian allies. They grouped their way along the footpath in a heavy rain and murky darkness, so that it was nearly sunrise when they reached the encampment of Half-King. From here the Half-King and his associate sachem, Scarooyada—orMonacatootha, conducted Washington to the tracks which had been discovered. Upon these he put two of his Indians, who followed them up like hounds and brought back word that they had traced them to a low bottom surrounded by rocks and trees, where the French were encamped, having built a few cabins for shelter from the rain.

A plan of attack was now determined upon to come upon them by surprise. Washington and his men formed on the right, Half-King and his men on the left, and with ghost-like silence they advanced to the brow of the ledge of rocks beneath which the French were encamped. Washington was in the advance, and as the French caught sight of him they flew to arms. A sharp fire ensued, which lasted for fifteen minutes, when the French gave way and ran. They were soon overtaken, and twenty-one prisoners taken. Washington's men on the right received the fire of the enemy. One man was killed and three wounded near Washington, the Indians sustaining no loss. The French had ten killed and one wounded. One, a bare-footed Canadian, named Mouceau, escaped and carried the tidings of the defeat to the Forks. Monsieur Jumonville, their commander, was shot through the head at the first fire, and his fate has been made the subject of lamentation in prose and verse. The Indians soon scalped the dead, and would have killed and scalped the prisoners had not Washington prevented them.

This battle, fought at daybreak on the morning of May 28, 1754, was the first in which Washington ever took a part; it was the initial battle which lost to the French so much of her possessions on America soil, and as Francis Parkman tersely put it, "in it was fired the first shot that set the world on fire." Washington, in writing of this occasion, said: "And, believe me, the whistling of the bullets had a most charming sound."

Jumonville was a native of Picardy, one of the old French provinces bordering on the English channel. His name was N. Coulon de Jumonville, and he was at the age of twenty-nine years, therefore seven years the senior of Washington. Early in life he came to Canada and married. He left a widow and one daughter. In 1755, one year after his death, the widow was pensioned in a small sum, and in 1775 the daughter, then grown to womanhood, took the veil as Charlotte Amiable.

Of the twenty-one prisoners taken at this engagement the two most important were an officer of some consequence, named Drouillion, and the subtle and redoubtable La Force. As Washington considered the latter an arch mischiefmaker, who had made considerable trouble at Venango the year previous, he now rejoiced to have him within his power. The prisoners were conducted to the camp at the Great Meadows, and from there, on the following day, were sent under a strong escort to Governor Dinwiddie, who was at Winchester, Virginia. They were treated with great courtesy by Washington, who furnished Drouillion and La Force with clothing from his his own scanty stock, and at their request gave them letters to the governor bespeaking for them the "respect and favor due their character and personal merit."

The Half-King was now fully aroused. He sent the scalps of the Frenchmen slain in the late skirmish, accompanied with black wampum and hatchets, to all his allies, summoning them to take up arms and join him at Redstone creek, "for their brothers, the English, had now begun in earnest." He went off to his home, promising to send down the river for all the Mingoes and Shawanees and to be back at the camp on the thirteenth with thirty or forty warriors accompanied by their wives and children. To assist him in the transportation of his people and their effects thirty men were detached, and twenty horses.

A pile of stones and a rude cross marked the grave of Jumonville until July 4th, 1908, when a tablet was erected bearing the following inscription:

Here lie the mortal remains
of
N. Coulon de Jumonville,
who in command of thrity-three French regulars, was surprised and killed in an engagement with Major

General Washington, in command of forty provincial troops, and Tannacharison, the Half-King, in command of a company of friendly Indians, on May 28, 1754.

This action was the first conflict at arms between the French and English for supremacy in the Mississippi valley.

Erected July 4th, 1908, under the auspices of the Centennial committee of 1904.

Washington's situation now was extremely perilous. Contrecoeur had finished the fort from which Ward had been driven. He had already nearly one thousand men with him, and reenforcements and Inidan allies were on their way to join him. Messengers sent by Jumonville previous to the late affray apprised him of the weakness of the encampment at the Great Meadows.

Washington lost no time in enlarging the entrenchments and erecting palisades. He wrote to Colonel Fry, who lay sick at Will's creek, having been seriously injured by his horse falling on him, urging immediate reenforcements,

Jumonville's Grave

but at the same time declaring his resolution to "fight with unequal numbers rather than give up one inch of what he had gained." The Half-King and Queen Aliquippa and twenty-five or thirty families, making in all eighty to one hundred Indians, arrived at the Great Meadows on June first.

Colonel Fry died on the thirty-first of May, a few days after the accident, and Major Muse took command and joined Washington, where he arrived on the ninth of June with the residue of the Virginia regiment and nine swivel guns, powder and balls. Major Muse had served with Laurence Washington in the campaign of the West Indies, and had been with him in the attack on Carthagena. He had been Washingtin's instructor three years before in the manual of arms, and was now acting as quartermaster. By the death of Colonel Fry the chief command devolved upon Major Washington, who was commissioned lieutenant-colonel on June fourth.

Captain James Mackaye, with an independent company of the royal army, composed of one hundred men from South Carolina, joined Washington on the tenth of June, bringing with him sixty beeves, five days' allowance of flour and some ammunition, but no cannon, as was expected. Captain Mackaye bearing a king's commission, could not receive orders from a provincial colonel, and camped separate from Washington's forces; neither would his men do work on the road, as it was not incumbent upon them as king's soldiers to perform such menial service. The force now encamped at the Great Meadows numbered about four hundred men.

Leaving Captain Mackaye with one company to guard the fort, to thus avoid mutiny and a conflict of authority, Washington and the rest of the force, on the sixteenth of June, pushed on over Laurel Hill, cutting the road with extreme labor, to Gist's plantation—a distance of about thirteen miles, consuming two weeks in the work, taking with him some wagons and the swivels.

On June twenty-seventh a detachment of seventy men under command of Captain Lewis was sent forward to clear the road from Gist's to the mouth of Redstone. Ahead of this was sent a party under Captain Polson, who were to reconnoitre. Meanwhile Washington completed his movements to Gist's.

Washington Retreats to the Great Meadows and Strengthens Fort Necessity.

On the twenty-ninth a council of war was held at Gist's at which it was determined to concentrate all the forces at this point, where some entrenchments had been already thrown up, with a view of making a stand. This entrenchment was near Gist's Indians' hut and a fine spring, and within fifty rods of the geographical center of Fayette county.

Captains Lewis and Polson were called in, and Captain Mackaye and his company were sent for. They all came, but upon receiving later news of the superior force of the French it was apparent that a stand here was inexpedient and that they should fall back as far as Will's creek and await reenforcements. The private baggage was left behind, and the horses of the officers were laden with ammunition and public stores. The soldiers of the Virginia regiment dragged the nine swivels by hand, the members of the independent company looking on and offering no aid. They reached the Great Meadows on the first day of July. Here the men were so exhausted by their labors and lack of nourishment that they could not draw their swivels nor carry their baggage on their backs any farther. They had been eight days without bread. They had milch cows for beef, but had no salt with which to season it, nor were the supplies which had been left at the stockade adequate to sustain the march. It was thought best, therefore, to here await both the supplies and reenforcements, having now but two poor teams and a few equally poor pack horses.

Washington immediately set his men to work to strengthen the fortifications, and under the supervision of Captain Stobo a ditch and additional dimensions and strength were given to the fort, which was now given the name of Fort Necessity on account of the extreme need of the troops.

Hearing of the arrival at Alexandia of two independent companies from New York some days before it was supposed that they might by this time have arrived at Will's creek, and a messenger was

Road over which Washington's men pulled the cannon by hand

dispatched to urge them up. Horses were hired to go to Will's creek for more ammunition and provisions, Gist endeavoring to have the artillery hauled out by Pennsylvania teams. It was ascertained that the two independent companies from New York and the one from North Carolina would fail to arrive until too late, and they only reached Will's creek after the surrender of Forty Necessity. No artillery came in time, only ten of the thirty four-pound cannon and carriages which had been sent from England reaching Will's creek until too late.

Besides the Indians already mentioned as crowding into the fort, many of the settlers with their families sought protection under the English arms. The warriors expected and promised by the Half-King from the Muskingum and Miami countries failed to join Washington.

From the time news reached Fort Duquesne of the defeat of Jumonville the greatest activity prevailed. On the twenty-eighth of June, just one month after that affair, a force of five hundred French and one hundred Indians, afterwards augmented to four hundred, left

Fort Duquesne under command of M. Coulon de Villiers, a half-brother to Jumonville, who sought the command as a special favor to enable him, as he termed it, to avenge the "assassination" of his kinsman.

De Villiers passed up the Monongahela on the thirtieth of June, and then moved on to Gist's settlement, a distance of about sixteen miles, reaching the place early the morning of the second of July. Opening fire upon the rude half-finished fort, and receiving no response, he found the place deserted. He thereupon prepared to return to Fort Duquesne, when a deserter arrived from Fort Necessity, who revealed the whereabouts and wretched condition of Washington's forces. He concluded to press on in pursuit of the English. He ascended the mountain by the road just opened by Washington, passed within five hundred wards of where his half-brother had fallen a little over a month before, and came within sight of Fort Necessity, after a rainy night, early on the morning of the third of July. He immediately delivered the first fire from the woods, at a distance of four or five hundred yards. The first position taken by the French was in the northwest, but afterwards they took position on the east and southeast, near the fort. Washington formed his men on the south, in the meadow outside the fort, in order to draw the enemy into an open encounter. Failing in this he retired behind the lines. The heavy rains the previous night had made the trenches untenable for Captain Mackaye's company. The French then took position on an eminence on the north, about sixty yards distant, and the Indians took position behinds trees and in tree tops. For nine hours, during a rain storm, the assailants poured an incessant shower of balls upon the little band crowded within the lines of the fort. The English replied with vigor, and toward six o'clock in the evening the conflict grew in animation, and continued until eight o'clock. Washington's tranquil presence encouraged his men and deceived the enemy.

Washington Makes His First and His Last Surrender.

De Villiers, fearing his ammunition would fail, proposed a parley, which Washington at first declined, but when repeated it was granted. The articles of capitulation were written in the French language, which, after sundry modifications in Washington's favor, were signed in duplicate—in the rain, by the light of a candle—by Captain James Mackaye, Lieutenant-Colonel George Washington and Coulon Villiers. According to the articles agreed to the garrison were allowed to remove all their belongings except the artillery and to march out with drums beating, and to have protection from insult or injury by the French or Indians. The English were to deliver up the officers, two cadets and the prisoners made at the defeat of Jumonville, and send them under safeguard to Fort Duquesne within two months and a half at the farthest. A duplicate of the articles was fixed upon one of the posts of the stockade. Jacob Van Braam and Robert Stobo, both captains, were delivered as hostages to the French officer as surety for the faithful compliance of the English to the articles of capitulation.

There were at the encampment at the Great Meadows at the time of the surrender about four hndred persons.

Personnel of the Officers Engaged.

M. Coulon de Villiers, captain of His Majest's troops, was a half-brother to Jumonville, and was of a family of seven brothers, six of whom lost their lives in the American wars. De Villiers was taken prisoner by the English at the capture of Fort Niagara in 1770.
Captain Mackaye assisted Colonel James Innes in the construction of Fort Cumberland, and afterward became one of the justices of the peace for Westmoreland county, Pa., and lived at Pittsburgh. He had been holding court at Hannastown and returned home on the ninth of April, 1774, and was arrested on the following day by Dr. Connelly under authority of the governor of Virginia. Connelly was holding court at Fort Dunmore under authority of Virginia, and Mackaye holding court at Hannastown under authority of Pennsylvania. He was sent, with other justices, to Staunton to be lodged in jail, but was permitted to go to Williamsburg, to present an account of his arrest and was allowed to return home. Colonel Mackaye was stationed at Kittanning to succeed Van

Swearingen at Fort Armstrong in July 20, 1776, with his battalion, and remained at that post until the fifteenth of December, when he was, against the remonstrances of the inhabitants, ordered elsewhere.

Captain Adam Stephens, to whom Washington gave a major's commission, became a captain in the Virginia regiment at Braddock's defeat and was wounded in the action at that time. He rose to be a colonel in the Virginia troops, and was with Grant at his defeat at Fort Duquesne. He became a brigadier general, and in February, 1779, was made a major general in the Revolutionary War. He was stationed at Fort Cumberland in November 1775, as lieutenant colonel by Governor Innes, of North Carlina, who had been in command at that place. While here there arose a dispute between Stephens and Captain Dagworthy as to rank, and Major General Shirley, who had succeeded Braddock in command of the colonies, had Dagworthy removed.

General Stephens was born about 1718 in Pennsylvania, and migrated to Virginia in 1738. He died in 1791 and was buried on his own plantation, a part of which is now embraced within the town limits of Martinsburg, Virginia.

Captain Robert Stobo was the only son of William Stobo, a merchant of Glasgow, in which city Robert was born in 1727. His father and mother both dying when he was young, he came to Virginia to serve in a store which was owned by some Glasgow merchants. He became a favorite of Governor Dinwiddie, who in 1754 appointed him the oldest captain of the Virginia regiment then raised. He was the engineer of Fort Necessity, and was one of the two hostages given up by Washington to be taken by the French to Fort Duquesne to be there held until the return of the French officers taken in the fight with Jumonville. The governor of Virginia refusing to comply with Washington's agreement and release the French officers, Stobo with Van Braam was sent to Canada. They were the first English military prisoners at Fort Duquesne. He was allowed much privilege as a prisoner until after the defeat of Braddock, when a great change was made in the treatment he received. The plans of

Fort Duquesne, an exact description of which he had forwarded to Governor Dinwiddie, and the information he had furnished, were captured among Braddock's effects and published. The consequences was that Stobo was ordered into close confinement. Subsequently he was tried and sentenced to be executed. The sentence was deferred, and at length he effected his escape and arrived at Louisburg, on the Island of Cape Breton, shortly after General Wolf had sailed for Quebec. He immediately returned to Quebec and afforded General Wolf much important information. He returned to Virginia in 1759, from whence he went to England. His heirs got an extra allowance of one thousand pounds and nine thousand acres of land in Kentucky for his services.

Captain Jacob Van Braam, as well as Adjutant Muse, had been a campaigning comrade of Lawrence Washington, and had been in the British army. He professed to be a complete master of fencing, and gave George Washington, when a youth, instructions in sword exercise. He was a Dutchman who knew a little French, and having served

Washington as a French interpreter the previous year on his mission to the forts on French creek, he was called upon to interpret the articles of capitulation at the surrender of Fort Necessity. It was through his stupidity as an interpreter that Washington was placed under the ban of an assassin by the French. For this blunder Van Braam was condemned of treachery by the House of Burgesses. He was given up by Washington to the French to be held as a hostage, along with Captain Stobo, until the return of the French officers taken at the defeat of Jumonville. By the refusal of Governor Dinwiddie to comply with Washington's agreement Van Braam was kept some time at Fort Duquesne and then sent to Quebec, along with Captain Stobo, where he was held until the conquest of Canada by the English. He returned to Virginia in 1760. He was awarded an allowance of five hundred pounds and nine thousand acres of land in Kentucky for his services.

Captain Andrew Lewis became a captain in Braddock's campaign, but had no command in the fatal action. He was with Major Grant in his defeat at Grant's

Hill in 1758. He became the General Lewis of Bottetourt in the great battle with the Indians at Point Pleasant in Dunmore's war of 1774, and was a distinguished general officer in the Revolution. It was he whom it was said Washington recommended for commander-in-chief of the American army.

Lieutenant William Polson became a captain in Braddock's campaign and was killed in the defeat. He was a native of Scotland.

Ensign Peyronie was a French Protestant chevalier, settled in Virginia, was badly wounded in the attack on Fort Necessity and became a Virginia captain in Braddock's campaign. He was killed on the field.

Dr. James Craik, a Scotchman by birth, but a resident of Alexandria, Virginia, had long been a friend and the family physician of Washington. He accompanied Washington as physician and surgeon from the beginning to the end of this campaign. He attended Colonel Fry, who died at Will's creek from injuries sustained by the falling of his horse. He was the companion of Washington when on his journey to the west in 1770, and was also his physician through his last illness. He entered the Revolutionary army as a surgeon and rose to the first rank. He was director-in-chief of the military hospital at Yorktown in 1781. He named one of his sons George Washington Craik, who became private secretary to President Washington in his second term. Dr. Craik was willed a chair and a desk, as mementoes, by Washington. Besides drawing his pay as both officer and surgeon in the campaign of 1754, Dr. Craik was awarded one thousand seven hundred and ninety-four acres of land. On the third of September, 1788, he obtained from Pennsylvania patent for two tracts of land in Franklin township, Fayette county, Pennsylvania. One was known as "Bowland's Camp," and the other as "Freeman's Sword," each containing four hundred and three acres. They were both sold the twenty-seventh of March, 1791, to Samuel Bryson. Dr. Craik died on his plantation, within five miles of Mt. Vernon, on the sixth of February, 1814.

Queen Aliquippa, with her son, lived at the confluence of the Youghiogheny with the Monongahela. She was an Indian squaw of some importance among her people, and received her royal title from the English. She became offended because Washington did not stop to see her on his way to the French forts in November, 1753, an offense for which he fully atoned on his return by presenting her with a few presents, among which the most highly prized was a bottle of rum.

Christopher Gist was of English descent. His grandfather, Christopher Gist, died in Baltimore county in 1691. His father, Richard Gist, was a surveyor; was one of the commissioners in 1729 for laying off the town of Baltimore, and was presiding magistrate in 1736. Christopher was one of three sons —Christopher, Thomas and Nathaniel, who all married sisters. Christopher had three sons—Nathaniel, Richard, Thomas—and two daughters, Nancy and Violet. He was a leading character of the times, being by nature an adventurer. In 1748 his residence was on the Yadkin, in North Carolina. He was employed by the "Ohio Company" in locating their grant of five hundred thousand acres of land on the Ohio river, the duties of which he performed in the years 1751 and 1752. On his return to his home in the former year he found the Indians had made an incursion into that settlement, had murdered many of his neighbors and burned the houses. His family had fled to the banks of the Roanoke, in Virginia, a distance of thirty-five miles. His residence was on the Yadkin river, and on the west side of a stream known as Sawmill creek, near and west of Reddie's river, near the present town of Wilkesbarre, in Wilkes county, North Carolina. He was residing at Will's creek when Washington secured his services as guide to the French posts, near Lake Erie, in November, 1753. On their way out and also on their return he stopped at Gist's new settlement at the western foot of Laurel Hill. Washington also spent the night with Gist at Will's creek on his return. With his sons, Nathaniel and Thomas, he was with Braddock on the fatal field, and for his services received a grant of twelve thousand acres of land from the king of England. He, with George Croghan, assisted in building the stockade at the Forks of the Ohio for the Ohio Company in 1754, and was purchasing agent for the Virginia soldiers stationed at Fort Mount Pleasant. After the defeat of Braddock, 1755 till 1765, he was engaged in various public capacities in the south and southwest. In the latter year he returned to his settlement west of the mountains, and after settling his family, he returned to his ,old home where he died of small-pox.

His son, Thomas Gist, remained at this new settlement until his death, in 1786, and was a man of considerable influence. Richard was killed at the battle of King's mountain. Nancy made her home with Thomas until his death, when she moved with her brother Nathaniel to their grant in Kentucky, where the family of Nathaniel Gist became quite prominent. Violet married William Cromwell, and lived on this new settlement.

What at that time was known as the Gist plantation was subsequently warranted by Virginia to Thomas Gist in right of Christopher Gist. There were five surveys made the twenty-sixth of October, 1785, aggregating two thousand, five hundred acres in one body. After the death of Thomas Gist this whole tract was sold to Colonel Isaac Meason, who gave it the name of Mt. Braddock. On this he erected a large stone mansion in 1802. His son, Isaac Meason, Jr., succeeded him in the possession of this farm, and after the death of the latter his widow sold it to Isaac Beeson.

Dr. Hugh Mercer was a Scotchman, having fled to Virginia from the service of the Pretender, on the fatal field of Culloden. He accompanied the Virginia troops as a surgeon. He also accompanied Braddock's army and was badly wounded on the fatal field. Being unable to escape in the general flight, he concealed himself behind a tree, from which place he was a forced witness to the scalping and plundering of the dead and dying. After darkness he left his hiding place and by the aid of the stars and streams, after several days of painful suffering, reached Fort Cumberland. He served as captain in Colonel Armstrong's expedition against the Indians at Kittanning, in 1756, from which he again returned severely wounded to Fort

Cumberland. He finally became a field officer in the Revolution and fell at Princeton in January, 1777.

The Proprietories of Pennsylvania, on March 2, 1771, granted to Dr. Hugh Mercer, of Fredericksburg, Virginia, two tracts of land, about three and a half miles from Stewart's Crossing, now in Bullskin township, Fayette county, containing two hundred and eighty-two and one-half, and three hundred and eleven acres respectively, and the usual allowance. These tracts were sold by the executors of Dr. Mercer to Isaac Meason the third of November, 1789.

Lieutenant Thomas Waggener, with his company, supported that of Washington at the attack on Jumonville, and these two companies received all the fire of the enemy. In this action he was wounded. He subsequently became a captain of the Virginia troops and as such accompanied Braddock in his campaign and displayed in that fatal action signal good sense and gallantry, and escaped unhurt.

Tanacharisson was a Seneca chief of great note, being head sachem of the mixed tribes which had migrated to the

Ohio and its tributaries. He was surnamed the Half-King, being subordinate to the Iroquois confederacy. Washington pronounced him a man of more than usual intelligence. In the spring of 1753, the Miami tribes under the leadership of Half-King, made a treaty at Carlisle with Benjamin Franklin, at which they plighted their friendship to the English. That Half-King proved faithful to his vow, history offers ample proof. His home was at Logstown, whense he accompanied Washington to the French forts in 1753. He was at the Forks of the Ohio when Ensign Ward surrendered that post, and vehemently protested against the conduct of the French commander on that occasion. He rendered invaluable service in the detection and defeat of Jumonville, and by his discretion and unswerving loyalty had won the admiration of Washington.

When Washington's little army retraced its steps over the mountains, Half-King took his family and went to Aughquick, in Pennsylvania, where they were maintained at the expense of the colony. A short time after his removal to Aughquick he was taken sick and in

October of this same year he died. His death was mourned with great lamentation by both the Indians and the whites.

Scarooyada succeeded him as sachem of the Delaware tribe. In April, 1755, the colony of Pennsylvania refused longer to support them and their destitute families. This treatment and that received at the hands of Braddock, created an antipathy in the breasts of the hitherto friendly Indians.

In this engagement it is reported that Washington lost thirty men killed and forty-two wounded. Captain Mackaye's loss was never reported. The French had two men killed and seventy wounded, two whereof were Indians.

By daylight the following morning the English flag was struck and the French flag took its place. The humiliated garrison took the situation as cheerfully as possible under the circumstances, and with banners flying and drums beating, the little army wended its way towards Will's creek. In its wake followed a retinue of settlers and adherents. The lilies of France now floated in undisputed victory over every fort, trading post and mission from the

Allegheny mountains westward to the Mississippi river. No sooner had the English garrison filed out of Fort Necessity than the French began its demolition. This accomplished to their gratification they began retracing their steps toward the mouth of Redstone the same day, for fear or re-enforcements as had been requested by Washington, and encamped about two leagues distant—perhaps at the Big Rock, where the Half-King had encamped the night before the attack on Jumonville. Doubtless DeVilliers turned aside and visited the spot where his half-brother had fallen and tenderly covered the remains with earth and stone to prevent their destruction by wild beasts and to mark the spot of their last resting place.

They reached the abandoned entrenchment at Gist's on the fifth, and after demolishing what was of it they burned all the contiguous houses. They reached the mouth of Redstone at ten o'clock next day, where they proceeded to burn the Hangard and then re-embarked on the Monongahela, returning to Fort Duquesne on the seventh.

Fort Necessity was in a glade between

two eminences, which were covered with forests, except within sixty yards of it. The road by which Washington's army had advanced passed within a few feet on the south, and Great Meadow run skirted the base line on the north.

The fort was in the form of an obtuse angled triangle of one hundred and five degrees, its base resting on Great Meadown run, about two perches of which were thrown across the stream and connected with the base by lines perpendicular to the opposite lines of the triangle. The base was eleven perches long, the western seven perches and the eastern line six perches. About fifty square perches of land, or nearly one-third of an acre, were included within these lines. The embankments in 1816 were still three feet high above the level of the meadow. The outside trenches, in which Captain Mackaye's men were stationed when the fight began, and from which they were flooded out, were already filled up, but inside the lines were ditches of about two feet in depth, formed by throwing the earth up against the palisades. It is eleven miles east of Union-

BRADDOCK'S EXPEDITIONS

town, and about eight hundred yards south of the national road.

The swivel cannon captured at the surrender, excepting the one allowed to be taken away by Washington's men, were left at the fort, where in after years they were found and used by emigrants for firing salutes. Eventually they were taken to Kentucky to be used by the settlers in defense against the Indians.

The night following the surrender Washington's army encamped barely three miles distant from the fort. It laboriously wended its way, the sick and wounded being carried by their fellows, to Will's creek, where the foremost arrived on the ninth.

Washington Retires to Mt. Vernon.

In 1752 the Ohio Company concluded to establish this as a permanent trading-post, although this point was eighty miles west of the frontier settlements. Here they erected another storehouse and magazine, which was known as the New Storehouse. This was located on the Virginia side of the Potomac, and was near the place now occupied by the abutment of the Potomac bridge. This structure was built of logs and was sufficiently commodious to accommodate a garrison and afford protection to settlers in case of an attack by Indians.

Washington proceeded to Williamsburg, where he made a full report of the campaign to Governor Dinwiddie, and after receiving a vote of thanks from the House of Burgesses for his bravery and gallant defense of his country, he retired to his home at Mount Vernon.

After Washington's return to Williamsburg Colonel James Innes, a Scotchman by birth, but a resident of North Caroline, marched to Will's creek and on the first of September, 1754, took command of that post, which had been garrisoned by Rutherford's and Clark's independent companies from New York. These had been sent to join Washington, but got no farther than Winchester.

Colonel Innes constructed a fort at the mouth of Will's creek, with the assistance of Captain Mackaye, beginning the twelfth of September and completing the work in about one month. This he named Fort Mount Pleasant. It was garrisoned during the winter of 1754-55. The

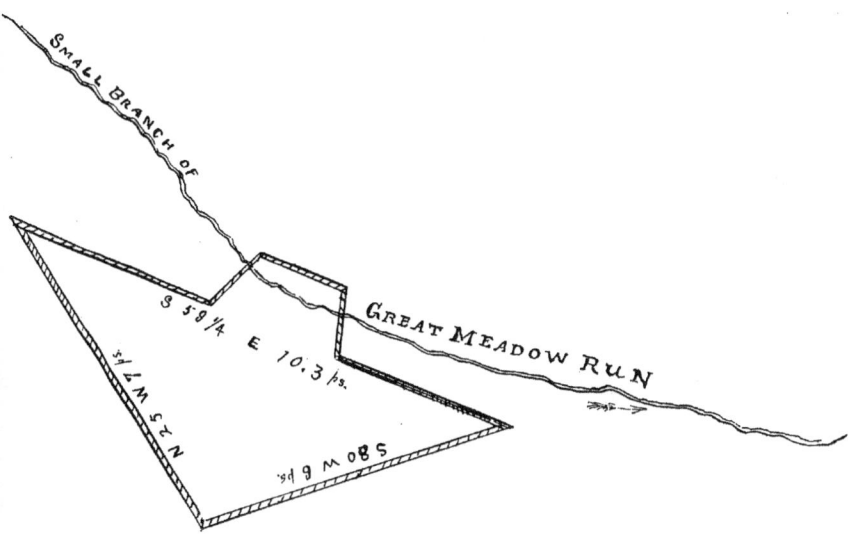

Fort Necessity as sketched by Freeman Lewis—1816

fort proper occupied almost the identical spot on which now stands the residence of James A. Milholland, known as the "Hoge house." This fort mounted four ten-pounders, besides swivels, and was favorably situated to keep the hostile Indians in check.

Washington Acquires a Title to the Site of Fort Necessity and Which He Held at the Time of His Death

As early as 1767 Washington acquired from Virginia a preempetion to a tract of land of three hundred and thirty-four acres under the name of Mt. Washington, which included the site of Fort Necessity. June 13, 1769, an application was sent in to the land office in right of William Brooks for three hundred acres called "Great Meadows," including an improvement made by a grant from Captain Charles Edmundstone, patented February 18, 1782, to General George Washington. The patent from the supreme Executive Council of Pennsylvania to General Washington recites that said tract of land was surveyed by virtue of an order issued June 13, 1769, by William Brooks, who by deed dated the seventeenth day of October, 1771, conveyed said tract of land and the appurtenances unto George Washington in fee simple, and a warant of acceptance of the survey issued to him, dated February 14, 1782. The consideration paid by Washington to the commonwealth of Pennsylvania was thirty-three pounds, fifteen shillings and eight pence, Pennsylvania money, which was some less than one hundred dollars.

This tract was referred to in his last will, and owned by him at the time of his death.

In December, 1776, the Virginia legislature proposed as adjustment to the boundary controversy that the western line of Maryland should be extended northward to the fortieth degree of latitude and thence westward along that parallel "until the distance of five degrees of longitude from the Delaware should be accomplished.' This would have thrown the site of Fort Necessity a distance of several miles within the territory of Virginia, but no formal action was taken on the part of Pennsylvania to this proposition. The running of the

Mason and Dixon line put an end to all controversy and secured to the Keystone state one of her cherished historic sites. After the death of Washington his executors sold it to Andrew Parks, of Baltimore, whose wife, Harriet, was a relative and legatee of Washington. She sold it to General Thomas Meason, who sold it to Joseph Huston, from whom it was sold to Colonel Samuel Evans for the taxes in 1824, and (it seems to have reverted back to Huston) sold as property of Huston by the sheriff to Honorable Nathaniel Ewing, who sold it to James Sampey, April 6, 1836, whose executors sold it to Godfrey Fazenbaker, December 29, 1856, for four thousand dollars. Mr. Fazenbaker's deed contained the following clause: "Excepting and reserving that piece heretofore conveyed by said executors to the Fort Necessity Washington Monument Association, with right of way and privileges, but if the conditions of the said asociation are not complied with the reservation is a nulity." Mr. Fazenbaker, however, agreed to extend the time almost indefinitely should the association continue its efforts to erect a monument at the old stockade.

Mr. Lewis Fazenbaker, the son of Godfrey Fazenbaker, is the present owner of the farm and says that the site of the fort has never been, nor never shall be, plowed over while it remains in the Fazenbaker name.

Washington owned at the time of his death over sixteen hundred acres of land in Franklin and Washington townships, on which was erected a flouring mill, which is still in operation. This tract of land was sold to Colonel Israel Shreeve.

An act of assembly was passed April 6, 1850, incorporating the Fort Necessity Washington Monument Association, making Daniel Sturgeon, John Washington, Samuel Y. Campbell, John Huston, Harvey Morris, Robert P. Flenniken, Andrew Stewart, Sebastion Rush, Daniel Kaine, Joshua B. Howell, William Stone, Zalmon Ludington and Isaac Beeson, of Fayette county, "and all other persons who have subscribed, or shall hereafter subscribe, any sum for the erection of a monument under the provisions of this act, and their successors or

Washington's Mill, built in Fayette County—1776

assigns, be and are hereby made a body corporate under the style of Fort Necessity Washington Monument Association, the property of this corporation to be forever exempt from taxation.

The first selection of officers was to be held the first Monday in May, 1850, and thereafter to be held on the twenty-second day of February each year. The board of managers held their first meeting at the house of Samuel Y. Campbell, May 6, 1850, but for lack of a quorum, agreed to meet at the office of R. P. Flenniken, Esq., Saturday, the eleventh. At this meeting Samuel Y. Campbell was elected president; Andrew Stewart, Harvey Morris, Joshua B. Howell, Samuel A. Gilmore and R. P. Flenniken, manager and Isaac Beeson, treasurer.

A committee, consisting of Andrew Stewart, Sebastian Rush, Samuel Y. Campbell and Thomas R. Davidson, was appointed to secure a title to one acre of ground, embracing the site of Fort Necessity, together with right of way thereto. Two agents were appointed in each township of the county to solicit subscriptions for the purchase of the ground and the erection of the monument. At a meeting of the managers, June twenty-second, Mr. Stewart presented the form of a deed of conveyance from the executors of James Sampey, conveying to the corporation one acre of ground, including the site of the fort, which form it was agreed should be executed.

Requests for contributions were sent to the President of the United States, the different heads of departments, the representatives in Congress from Pennsylvania, Maryland, Virginia and South Carolina, the literary institutions of the state, the governor, and to Major Delafield and cadets of West Point, the Masonic and Odd Fellow lodges and encampments of the state.

An effort was made March 2, 1852, to have the Topographical Department at Washington appoint a gentleman of the department to visit the site of Fort Necessity and make a drawing, as near as circumstances would permit, of the original stockade for the purpose of having the same lithographed, to be used as an inducement for subscriptions.

On August 6, 1851, Captain F. Clarke,

BRADDOCK'S EXPEDITIONS

who was then at Brownsville, was written to and solicited to visit the site and make a draft of the location and environs. On August 14, 1851, Captain K. Dawson was also requested to make a draft of the same.

Agents were sent out to canvass Fayette and neighboring counties for subscriptions. Some little money was obtained; some of the solicitors proved to be defaulters, and what funds did find their way to the treasury were consumed in stationery, postage and clerical work. So, after several months of heroic effort in a noble cause the Fort Necessity Washington Monument Association was doomed to die a lingering death.

In 1854, J. N. H. Patrick, Esq., editor of the Democratic Sentinel of Uniontown, Pa., urged a celebration to be held on the Fourth day of July of that year with a view of making a move toward the erection of a monument at the site of the old stockade. Lodge No. 228 A. Y. M. of Uniontown and a large concourse of citizens visited the place and conducted suitable ceremonies, and a corner stone was placed near the center of the enclosure. David Shriver Stewart, son of Hon Andrew Stewart, performed the last named ceremony.

Not long after the corner was laid the contents, whatever they may have been, were removed, and some six years ago the upper stone was pried from its position, broken in two and left on the surface of the ground, a sad reminder of the vandalism liable to be perpetuated on any sacred object. The embankments have been worn down in the lapse of years until they are scarcely larged than a furrow thrown up with a plow yet much of the outlines can be easily traced.

In January, 1899, Hon. T. Robb Deyarmon, of Fayette county, introduced in the lower House a bill entitled, "An act providing for the acquisition by the state of certain grounds at Fort Necessity, Fayette county, and making an appropriation of ten thousand dollars therefor." This bill got as far as the committee on appropriations, and there was buried in oblivion.

A magnificent and patriotic celebration was held on the site of Fort Necessity, July 4th, 1904, in commemoration of the one hundred and fiftieth anniversary of the surrender of that fort.

BRADDOCK'S EXPEDITIONS

The patriotic sentiment of the citizens of Fayette county was aroused when Fort Necessity Lodge of I. O. O. F. took the iniative in a celebration of the one hundred and fiftieth anniversary of the surrender of Fort Necessity. Pressing invitations were sent throughout Fayette and adjoining counties, urging that an enthusiastic meeting be held at the site of the old fort and that patriotic addresses appropriate to the occasion be made.

The suggestion met with a most happy response, and upon the day of the occasion, long before daylight, the roads leading to this historic spot was crowded with vehicles and persons on foot.

A grand parade was formed on the National Road under Chief Marshal Lieutenant Colonel Everhart Bierer and his aide, M. A. Keifer, followed by Rutter's Silver Cornet Band, Co. C of Uniontown under command of Capt. A. G. Beeson, Co. D of Connellsville under command of Capt. John L. Gans, Uniontown Fire Department, Co. A Boys Brigade under Lieut. Chas. Hall, Co. E under Sergeant Maj. L. S. Sloan, Co. F under First Sergeant Jay W. Johns, Co. G under First Lieut. Ralph C. Kennedy and all under the command of Adjutant I. E. Keener.

Next came the Soldiers' orphans from the Jumonville Soldiers' Orphan school under the care of Superintendent John A. Waters, Fort Necessity Lodge I. O. O. F., followed by a cavalcade most imposing.

It is estimated that fully 8,000 people participated in the celebration of the occasion, and it can be truthfully stated that not the slightest disorder marred the enjoyment of the day.

The officers of this celebration committee were, President, Hon. E. H. Reppert, Secretary, James Hadden, Treasurer, M. H. Bowman. These were ably assisted by not only many of the prominent citizens of the town but throughout the county.

The meeting at the grove was presided over by Hon. E. H. Reppert who introduced the speakers. Rev. F. E. J. Lloyd of the Episcopal church pronounced the invocation, after which Judge Reppert made some happy introductory remarks and then introduced Robert F. Hopwood who read the Declaration of Independence. Hon. George C. Sturgis of Morgantown, West Virginia delivered a most able and patriotic address. He was followed by Rev. Father A. A. Lambing of Wilkinsburg. The next speaker was Judge F. G. White of Pontiac, Ill.

Letters of regret from Senator P. C. Knox Hon. Hampton L. Carson, Hon. J. P. Dolliver, Hon. Lott Thomas, John W. Beazell, Hon. Boyd Crumrine, Dr. T. N. Boyle, Dr. C. W. Smith, Dr. Camden M. Coburn and Gen. M. I. Ludington were read by John S. Ritenour, and the benediction was pronounced by Rev. W. H. Gladden of the M. P. church of Connellsville.

The services at the grove were enjoyed to the utmost by the vast throng who gave the speakers most respectful attention.

A most bountiful dinner was served in the grove, after which a sham-battle took place between the troops, and another between the members of the boys' brigade all of which was greatly enjoyed by the spectators.

The site of Fort Necessity remained unmarked until July 4th, 1908, when a tablet was erected thereon bearing the following instcription:

This tablet marks the site
of
Fort Necessity
where Lieutenant Colonel George Washington, in command of four hundred provincial troops, after an engagement of nine hours, capitulated to M. Coulon de Villiers, in command of nine hundred French regulars and their Indian allies, on July 4th, 1754.

Washington lost 30 men killed and 42 wounded. Captain Mackaye's loss was never reported. The French had two men killed and 70 wounded, two whereof were Indians.

Erected July 4th, 1908, under the auspices of the Centennial Celebration committee of 1904.

General Edward Braddock

CHAPTER II.

Expedition of Major General Edward Braddock Against the French at Fort Duquesne, 1755.

Edward Broddock was born in Perthshire, Scotland, about 1695, and was the only son of Major General Braddock. He entered the army as ensign in the Grenadier company, second regiment of the Coldstream Guards, on the eleventh of October, 1710, at the age of fifteen years. This was a very aristocratic division of the British army, and the bodyguard of royalty. From this his promotions were rapid.

On the twenty-fifth of November, 1754, Major General Edward Braddock was commissioned general-in-chief of His Majesty's forces in North America and received his instructions concerning his duties in relation to the encroachments of the French. Becoming impatient of the preparation of the troops he set sail from Cork aboard the "Norwich" on the twenty-first of December, 1754, and arrived at Alexandria, Virginia, February 20, 1755. His troops—the Forty-fourth regiment, under Colonel Sir Peter Halket, and the Forty-eighth regiment, under Colonel Dunbar—set sail on the fourteenth of January and landed in March, 1755, and marched to Alexandria. These regiments were of the royal troops, and numbered five hundred men each.

A council was held at Alexandria on the fourteenth of April, at which were present Honorable Augustus Keppel, commander-in-chief of His Majesty's ships, and the governors of Massachusetts, Virginia, New York, Pennsylvania and Maryland. Here three expeditions were planned, one of which was to be under the command of General Braddock with the British troops, with such aid as might be derived from Maryland and Virginia, to which were afterward added two independent companies from New York.

General Braddock was to move against the French at Fort Duquesne, and from thence to Canada. With this object in view he marched from Alexandria the twentieth of April, and reached Fredericktown, Maryland, on the twenty-fourth. Passing through Winchester he reached Fort Mount Pleasant on the ninth of May, to which point Sir John Sinclair, deputy quartermaster general, had preceded him about two weeks. General Braddock, having been designated by the Duke of Cumberland the captain general of the British army, requested of Governor Dinwiddie that the name of the new fort be changed from Fort Mount Pleasant to that of Fort Cumberland, by which name it was ever afterward known. Here, on the 10th of May, Washington was appointed aide-de-camp to His Excellency, Major General Braddock.

Braddock's army now consisted of the Forty-fourth regiment, English infantry, Col. Sir Peter Halket; the Forty-eighth, Col. Thomas Dunbar; sundry independent colonial companies, a company of horse, a company of artillery, a company of marines, etc. The two independent companies of New York, under command of Captains Rutherford and Gates, the latter to whom Burgoyne surrendered at Saratoga, had garrisoned the fort during the winter of 1754-55. The field officers were Lieut. Cols. Burton and Gage, the latter of Bunker Hill notoriety; Majors Chapman and Sparks, Major Sir John Sinclair, quartermaster general; Matthew Leslie, his assistant; Capt. Robert Orme, of the Coldstream Guards; Christopher Gist and his son Nathaniel as guides; Drs. James Clark and Hugh Mercer. These had been with Washington in his campaign the previous year.

Braddock was here tendered the valuable services also of George Croghan, the Indian agent of Aughwick; Montour, the Indian diplomatist; Monacatootha, the successor of Half-King, whose acquaintance and friendship Washington had formed when on his mission to Le Boeuf, with about 150 Seneca and Delaware Indians, and Captain Jack with his company of warriors and scouts. These offered their services without pay and to furnish their own arms, all on conditions that they were to dress, march and fight as they pleased and to be free from strict military discipline.

With such a strict disciplinarian as Braddock such conditions could not for

Fort Cumberland—1755

one moment be considered and the offer was peremptorily refused, whereupon Captain Jack with his band, together with nearly every Indian, turned upon his heel in disgust and marched back to the hills of the Juniatta.

Had Braddock accepted the services of these experienced warrors and scouts the result of his expedition can only now be conjectural, but the consequence of his refusal and of his strict adherence to military discipline history has amply recorded.

Captain Jack, who was also known as "Susquehanna Jack," "The Black Rifle," "The Black Hunter," and "The Wild Hunter of the Juniata," was a large, powerful and fearless frontier settler of the valley of the Juniata, through whose veins ran a goodly mixture of Indian if not a baser blood.

Once upon returning from a long and weary chase he was horrified to find his cabin in ashes and the corpses of his murdered family scattered around. From this time to the day of his death his thirst for Indian blood could never be satisfied. His fame as an Indian fighter soon spread from the head springs of the Susquehanna to the Potomac.

The old pathway along which Captain Jack traveled, and in which he met his dusky foe in mortal combat, and in which so many fell a victim to his deadly rifle, is still plainly visible.

His bones respose in a lonely grave near his favorite spring at the base of the mountain which bears his name and stands as a towering monument to perpetuate his memory.

Reference has frequently been made to a monument that stands in the Falling Spring cemetery at Chambersburg, Pa., which bears the following inscription: "Colonel Patrick Jack, an offcer of the Colonial and Revolutionary wars, died January 25th, 1829, aged 91 years."

This latter was not the Captain Jack who offered his services to Braddock, but was a resident of Chambersburg at the time of his death.

Monacatooths, known also as Scarooyada, with a few of his followers, not more than eight in number, however, followed Braddock through the campaign and rendered valuable service. At a council held at Onondago by the Six

BRADDOCK'S EXPEDITIONS 73

Nations, Monacatootha had been selected to succeed Tanacharisson or Half-King, as sachem. The clever pencil of the artist could not throw upon canvass a more dignified specimen of the noble race. The majestic form of this warrior as it towered above his followers leading the van, followed by the glittering array of the first disciplined army whose martial tread ever awoke the echoes of these primeval forests, was grand in the extreme. His leggings were frilled with locks from the dried scalps of his conquered foes; his own scalp lock, plaited down his back, a well understook token of defiance, over which waved the plume feathers of the eagle, the emblem of American liberty, was further gaudily ornamented with the gorgeous plumage of the blue jay. On his noble breast was plainly tattooed a tomahawk, the emblem of war, and on each cheek he bore the signs of the hunter, the bow and arrow.

The army had marched but a little over twenty miles from Fort Cumberland when Monacatooths, who was a little in advance, was surrounded and taken by some French and Indians. The former were determined to put him to death but the latter remonstrated and even threatened to join the English should the French carry out their design. The sachem was then lashed to a tree and left to his fate, but fortunately was soon found and released by his son and other Indians.

While the army was encamped at Thicketty Run, July 4th, two of Monacatootha's men were sent to reconnoiter and returned with the scalp of a French officer which they had succeeded in taking within half a mile of the fort.

On July 6th, while the army was on the march from Thicketty Run, by a disregard of a preconcerted signal, Manacatootha's son was fired upon and killed by some outrangers of Braddock's army. The general displayed great sorrow for the unfortunate occurrence and after due expressions of sympathy and donations caused the body to be buried in the honors of war at the next encampment, which also received the name of "Monacatootha" in honor of the bereaved sachem.

The Colonial Records and the Pennsylvania Archives bear ample evidence that this noble sachem not only held a commission under the province of Pennsylvania, but that his mature judgment was sought in the deliberations of the councils of the same.

Braddock's whole force amounted to about 2150 men at Fort Cumberland. But by haughtily rejecting the proffered services of the Indians as scouts and guides, many of them retired to the mountains of the Juniata. Scarooyada and a few others, however, followed Braddock throughout the campaign. This sachem afterward, in a speech at Philadelphia, denounced the French as cowards and the English as fools.

Braddock at this time had under his command several officers, both white and Indian, who were far more competent to command than he, and who, if permitted the opportunity, would doubtless have led the troops to victory.

On the 27th of May Sir John Sinclair and Major Chapman were sent forward with a detachment of 500 men to widen the road opened by Washington the previous year, to advance as far as the Little Meadows and there erect a fort and collect provisions. On the 7th of June the first division, under Sir Peter Halket, moved forward and on the 8th the second division, under Lieut. Col. Gage, of the Forty-fourth, and on the the 10th the main body of the army, with the commander-in-chief left Fort Cumberland.

Through the influence of Dr. Benjamin Franklin 150 wagons and 2000 horses joined Braddock on the 8th of June, and the army was enabled to move. The first camp was called "Camp at the Grove," and from here orders were issued, and the commander-in-chief rested till the 12th. He encamped at "Martin's" on Saturday, June 14th. The army was seven days in reaching the Little Meadows, a distance of twenty miles from Fort Cumberland. Here a council was held, at which it was determined that Gen. Braddock, with 1200 men and 12 pieces of cannon, should press on, leaving Colonel Dunbar and Major Chapman to follow by easy stages. At the Little Crossings, two miles west of the Little Meadows, Washington was taken down with a fever and was left under the care of Dr. Craik and a guard to await the arrival of Colonel Dunbar, who came up in two days. Washington had exacted, however, from Braddock, a

BRADDOCK'S EXPEDITIONS 77

promise not to make the attack on Fort Duquesne until he came up. The army reached the Great Crossings, a distance of 17 miles further west, on the 23rd.

The first encampment on Fayette county soil was at the "Twelve Springs," having marched from Squaw's Fort, near the Big Crossings, six miles. This encampment was between what is now known as Mount Augusta and Marlow's, and south of the National road. Here the army encamped the 24th.

On the 25th the army made a memorable march. Within about a quarter of a mile after starting a bluff was reached over which it was necessary to let down the carriages by the use of ropes and tackle. During the day's march three men were killed and scalped by the enemy, and some French and Indians were fired upon by the sentinels.

The Site of Fort Necessity Passed Without Notice.

The ruins of Fort Necessity were passed without halt or seeming notice, and the army camped about two miles beyond the Great Meadows after a march of seven miles. This encampment is known as the "Old Orchard" camp, and was reached late in the day. There may have been some superstitious belief which caused Braddock to pass the Great Meadows without a halt.

Nothing was further from the proud commander's mind while encamped at this place than the thought that within a little more than a fortnight the same should witness the disordered retreat of the remnant of his defeated army, should hear his dying moans and be his sepulcher, but such it proved to be.

The following day (26th) Braddock offered a bounty of five pounds for every scalp that his Indians and soldiers should take. On account of the roughness of the road the march was a distance of four miles only. This encampment was known as "Rock Fort" or "Great Rock," and was near a fine spring, now known as Washington's Spring. The rock was situated on the crest of Laurel Hill, and near the same as occupied by Half-King the year before, when he notified Washington of the approach of Jumonville's party. Here they found another Indian camp, which had just been deserted. The fire was still burning, and a commission was found indicating that the party was under the command of Sieur Normanville.

From "Rock Fort" the army marched on the 27th northward along the crest of Laurel Hill, passing within a few hundred feet of the scene of Jumonville's defeat, and to the eastward of the prominence, at the western foot of which was lately located the Jumnoville Orphan school, and encamped at Gist's plantation, where Washington had commenced a stockade the year before, a distance of some eight miles from "Rock Fort."

On the 28th the army marched to the Youghiogheny and encamped at Stewart's crossing, a short distance below where the town of Connellsville now stands. The crossing was effected on the 30th, and the army pursued a northeasterly course and passed about a mile and a half below where the town of Mount Pleasant now stands, and west of Greensburg to Bush fork of Turtle Creek. Here Braddock left the Nemacolin trail and turning to the westward encamped about two miles distant from the Monongahela river. Here Washington joined him on the evening of July 8th, he having come forward with a detachment of 100 men with packhorses and provisions on July 3d, and was hauled to this place in a covered wagon.

At 3 o'clock on the morning of July 9th Col. Thomas Gage led the advance and crossed to the west bank of the Monongahela by 8 o'clock, with a body of 300 men. He was immediately followed by another body of 200 men. Next came the general with the column of artillery, the main body of the army and the baggage. This crossing was near the site of the present town of McKeesport. The army then marched down three miles and halted to take dinner. Washington describes the march and manoeuvers of the army at this place to be the grandest sight he had ever beheld. The recrossing was effected just below the mouth of Turtle Creek, and by 1 o'clock the whole had recrossed the river.

The Assault.

Almost at this moment a sharp fire was heard upon the advance party, under Col. Gage, who was now ascending the

Braddock's Battlefield

hill about 100 yards from the terminus of the plain. A heavy fire of musketry was poured in upon his troops by an invisible foe. The fire was returned at random, consequently to no effect. The advance became panic stricken and fell back, the officers all the while trying in vain to cause a rally and restore order. For nearly three hours the troops huddled together in confusion in the narrow pass and were being shot down by the enemy hidden in the ravines on each side. The Virginia provincials, understanding the Indian mode of warfare, would have taken to the trees and routed the enemy had Braddock permitted. He denounced them as cowards and dastards for treeing, and even struck many of them down with his sword, an act for which he soon paid the penalty, as the sequel will show.

In the confusion of the battle more than half of the whole army was either killed or wounded, two-thirds of them being shot down by their own men. Braddock had four horses killed under him and at last, while on the fifth, he received a mortal wound which shattered his right arm and penetrated his lungs.

He was carried from the field. Had it not been for the devotedness of his aide, Capt. Orme, and the fidelity of Capt. Stewart, of Virginia, who was in command of the light horse, the fallen general would have had his wish gratified, "that the scene of his disaster would also witness his death." He was wrapped in a silken sash taken from about his waist, which English officers were wont to carry, and was carried off the field by his faithful body servant, Bishop, whom, in his dying moments, he bequeathed to Washington.

The silken sash in which he was borne from the field was kept, and after the Mexican war was presented to Gen. Zachary Taylor from whom it descended to his daughter, Mrs. Betty Dandridge, in whose possession it remained until her death.

The Deadly Result.

Out of eighty-nine commissioned officers twenty-six were killed and thirty-seven wounded, and of the soldiers 430 were killed and about 400 wounded. the killed being in excess of the wounded. Every field officer, and every one on horseback, except Washington, who had two horses killed under him and four bullets through his coat, was either killed or carried off the field wounded. Washington that day rode upon a pillow, so enfeebled and emaciated was he from the attack of fever; and yet, with great coolness, at the head of the provincials, he formed and covered the retreat.

Sir Peter Halket and the gallant young secretary, Shirley, were among the killed. Captain Orme saved his journal, which is now so highly prized as being an authentic and continuous record of this unfortunate campaign. All the artillery, ammunition, baggage and store, together with the dead and the dying were left on the fatal field. All the secretary's papers, with all the commanding general's orders, instructions and correspondence, together with the military chest, containing twenty-five thousand pounds in money, fell into the hands of the French. The Pennsylvania wagoners escaped to a man on their fleetest horses, some arriving at Dunbar's camp, a distance of 40 miles, by 10 o'clock the next morning, and one or two wounded officers were carried into camp before noon of this same day.

The French Contingent.

M. de Contrecour was in chief command at Fort Duquesne, under whom were De Beaujeu and Charles de Langdale. De Beaujeu, at the head of a force of 250 French and 650 Indians, marched out of Fort Duquesne at 9 o'clock on the morning of July 9th, and by half past twelve o'clock found himself in the presence of the English. De Beaujeu fell early in the battle and soon expired, and Dumas being next in command, led the attack after De Beaujeu fell. The loss of the French was slight, but fell chiefly on the officers, three of whom were killed and four wounded. Of the regular soldiers all but four escaped unwounded. The Canadians suffered still less in proportion to their number. The Indians, who won the victory, bore the principal loss.

The remnant of Braddock's defeated army attempted to make a rally on the west side of the river to await reinforcements from Col. Dunbar, but in this they utterly failed. The Indians made no attempt to pursue the retreating army, but contented themselves with scalping and pillaging the dead. From this place Washington was ordered on to Dunbar for wagons, provisions and hospital stores. He rode all night in the rain and darkness and reached Dunbar at daybreak.

Braddock was borne on a litter and reached Gist's plantation by 10 o'clock the next evening and lay at the Indian's spring that night awaiting surgical aid from Dunbar. Early in the night succeeding the battle many reached the deserted settlement of Gist. Here they met wagons and provisions with Washington and a detachment of soldiers from Dunbar. These Braddock ordered to proceed to the relief of the stragglers still left behind.

Sir John Sinclair was borne into Dunbar's camp on the 10th, on a sheet, and Braddock was moved up the following day. Col. Dunbar, with Major Chapman, had been left at the Little Meadows, to follow on by easy stages with the heavy ordnance and supplies. They passed Fort Necessity on the 2nd of July, and formed his final encampment on the summit of Laurel Hill, a flat piece of land in close proximity to a fine spring, and within a few hundred yards of the fatal action with Jumonville.

The panic-stricken fugitives came pouring into the encampment of Dunbar; the drums beat to arms, the fright became contagious, and disorder reigned supreme. By order of Braddock barrels of powder, amounting to 50,000 pounds, were staved and the contents thrown into a pool which had formed below the spring; the shells were bursted and about 150 wagons were burned to prevent them falling into the hands of the enemy. Col. Dunbar, in his report to Governor Shirley, states positively that there was not a gun of any kind buried. Many balls, bayonets and pieces of shells have been gathered up from the camp, and scarcely a museum of the state but contains many specimens. One collector has in his possession the half of a forty-pound shell which was made for an eight-inch gun, and two solid shot weighing 12 pounds each. These bear the English mark of the "Broad Arrow."

Since the removal of the Soldiers'

Dunbar's Encampment

Orphan school to the immediate neighborhood of the camp, in 1875, there have been collected enough pieces of shell and balls from which two small cannons were moulded. These weigh about 200 pounds each. One is in Pittsburg and the other is mounted and kept at the school, where it is used for firing salutes. One of these small cannons was presented to the Abe Patterson Post No. 88 G. A. R., of Allegheny City. It was mounted on lumber taken from Perry's fleet.

The retreat from Dunbar's camp was begun on the 13th, and by the same route as the advance had been made. An encampment was made at the Old Orchard, the same place as Braddock had encamped on his way out. Braddock was silent all the first day after the defeat, and at night only said: "Who would have thought it?" All the next day he he was again silent, till at last he muttered: "We shall know better how to deal with them the next time," and died in a few minutes after. Before breathing his last the dying general bequeathed his favorite charger and his body servant, Bishop, to Washington in recognition of his faithfulness as a staff officer.

88   WASHINGTON'S AND

General Braddock's Death and Burial.

General Braddock died on Sunday evening about 8 o'clock, July 13, 1755. He was wrapped in his cloak as a winding sheet and buried at daybreak on Monday morning, at the camp, in the middle of the road, that the army in passing over the grave might obliterate every trace of its whereabouts, and thus avoid any desecration of the body by the Indians. The chaplain having been wounded, Washington read the Episcopal funeral service, and the dead general was buried with the honors of war. A few days after the retreat of Dunbar the French sent out a party who advanced as far as the deserted camp, and proceeded to complete the destruction of everything destructible that could be found.

Braddock's Slayer.

It has always been related that one Thomas Fossit fired the fatal shot that caused the death of General Braddock. Fossit was a soldier in Captain Cholmondeley's company, having enlisted at Shippensburg, Pa. He was a large man, of great strength, rude habits and strong passions. He had a brother Joseph who was also in the same company. In the engagement at Braddock's field the provincials took to the trees, in Indian fashion, and were doing good execution, but Braddock cursed them as dastards and cowards and cut many of them down with his sword. Tom Fossit saw the reckless general cut his brother down, and this was more than a man of his temperament could endure. He sought and obtained revenge. Fossit took up a tract of 100 acres of land at the junction of Braddock's and Dunlap's roads on the summit of Laurel Hill. This included the site of "Rock Fort" or "Big Rock" and "Washington Springs." Here he kept a tavern for several years. He sold his rights to this tract April 29, 1788, to Isaac Phillips for the sum of fifty pounds. This stand was afterward known as Slack's tavern, and was considered a good stand until the National road was opened over the mountains. In October, 1816, Fossit was a pauper at Thomas Mitchell's, in Wharton township, and claimed then to be 104 years of age. He made his final home with Thomas Stewart, not far distant from Ohio Pyle, and at whose home he died at the remarkable age of 109 years. When intoxicated he would often relate the scenes of Braddock's defeat, and in obscure language hint to the circumstances of firing the fatal shot. He was said to have been married three times, and that two of his wives were killed by the Indians, and that his favorite, as he termed his "little Dutch wife,' was tomahawked before his eyes. He died about 1820.

The Continued Retreat.

The retreating army encamped at Little Meadows the following night after Braddock's death, a distance of 32 miles from Old Orchard camp. Col Dunbar arrived at Fort Cumberland by the 18th of July, and remained there until the 2nd of August. While here he was met with earnest requests from the governors of Pennsylvania, Maryland and Virginia that he would post his troops on the frontier so as to afford some protection to the inhabitants. To all these entreaties Dunbar turned a deaf ear, and continued his hasty march through the country, not considering himself safe until he arrived at Philadelphia.

The Scattered Army.

Washington remained at Fort Cumberland for a few days, being in feeble health and still suffering from the effects of his illness. While here he wrote the following letter to Governor Dinwiddie:

Fort Cumberland, July 18, 1755.
Honorable Sir:—
As I am favored with an opportunity, I should think myself inexcusable were I to omit giving you some account of our late action with the French on the Monongahela, the 9th instant. We conducted our march from Fort Cumberland to Frazer's, which is about seven miles from Fort Duquesne, without meeting any extraordinary event, having only a straggler or two picked up by the French Indians. When we came to this place we were attacked (very unexpectedly I must own) by about 300 French and Indians. Our number consisted of about 1300 chosen men, well armed, chiefly regulars who were immediately struck

with such a deadly panic that nothing but confusion and disobedience of orders prevailed among them. The officers in general behaved with incomparable bravery, for which they greatly suffered, there being nearly 60 killed and wounded, a large proportion out of the number we had.

Our poor Virginians behaved like men and died like soldiers, for I believe out of three companies that were there that day scarce 30 were left alive. Capt. Polson shared almost as hard a fate, for only one of his escaped; in short the dastardly behavior of the English soldiers exposed all those that were inclined to do their duty to almost certain death, and at length, in despite of every effort, broke and ran like sheep before the hounds, leaving the artillery, ammunition and provisions and every individual thing amongst us as a prey for the enemy; and when we endeavored to rally them, in hopes of regaining our invaluable loss, it was with as much success as if we had attempted to stop the wild boars on the mountains.

The General was wounded behind the shoulder and in the breast, of which he died the third day after. His two aids-de-camp were both wounded, but are in a fair way of recovery. Col. Burton and Sir John Sinclair were also wounded and I hope will get over it.

Sir Peter Halket, with many other brave officers, was killed on the field. I. luckily, escaped without a wound, though I had four bullets through my coat and two horses shot under me.

It is supposed we left 300 or more dead on the field; about that number we brought off wounded, and it is imagined, with great notice too, that two-thirds of both these numbers received their shots from our own cowardly dogs of soldiers who gathered themselves into a body, contrary to orders, ten or twelve deep; would then level and fire and shoot down the men before them.

I tremble at the conseqeunce this defeat may have on the back inhabitants, who I suppose will all leave their habitations unless proper measures are taken for their security. Col. Dunbar, who commands at present, intends as soon as his men are recruited at this place, to continue his march to Philadelphia into winter quarters, so that there will be none left here unless the poor remains of the Virginia troops who now are and will be too small to guard our frontier.

As Capt. Orme is now writing to your Honor I doubt not that he will give you a circumstantial account of all things which will made it needless for me to add more than that I am, Honorable Sir,

Your most humble servant,

Geo. Washington.

He then retired to Mt. Vernon, where he arrived on the 26th day of July. Col. Dunbar returned to England, where in November following he was suspended because of his injudicious retreat, and was sent into honorable retirement as lieutenant governor of Gibraltar. He was never again actively employed, and died in 1777.

By the defeat of Braddock and the withdrawal of the troops the frontiers of Pennsylvania, Maryland and Virginia were left in unutterable gloom. The most westward forts were Fort Cumberland and Fort Ligonier, and behind these the inhabitants shut themselves far east of their western boundaries. This condition of affairs continued until in November, 1758, when Brig. Gen. John Forbes crossed the moutains at Ligonier and settled forever the dispute for the Ohio Valley.

Some of the Participants.

One Samuel Jenkins, who was born a slave and was the property of Captain Broadwater, of Fairfax county, Virginia, drove a provision train over the mountains in the Braddock campaign. He died in Lancaster, Ohio, on the 4th of February, 1849, at the advanced age of 115 years. He doubtless was the last survivor of this ill-fated campaign.

Owen Davis was the owner and driver of a team in this expedition. He settled on George Creek, where he built a mill, which he replaced by a far better one in 1795. This mill was erected very near the site of what is recently known as the Ruble mill. Mr. Davis died December 22, 1809, in the 85th year of his age, and was buried on his farm, near the Ruble mill.

Sir John Sinclair was shot through the body and carried to Fort Cumberland.

He afterward fully recovered and accompanied Gen. Forbes in his expedition against Fort Duquesne, and the very best eulogy that general could pass upon Sir John was that "his only talent was for throwing everything into confusion." One other accomplishment might have been mentioned, that "he could, on the least provocation, use the vilest and most profane language."

Sir Peter Halket, of Pitcairn, had ominous forebodings as to the result of the coming conflict, and had earnestly pressed upon his general the importance of guarding against an ambuscade. He was captain of the 44th regiment of foot and was in command of the First Brigade. In the engagement he was killed from his horse while directing the movements of his men. Two of his sons were fighting under his command, one of which, Lieutenant James Halket, hastened at the moment to his aid, and, bending to raise the prostrate form, he too was pierced by a bullet from the invisible foe and fell dead across the prostrate form of his father.

When Brig. Gen. John Forbes marched his army out in the fall of 1758 against Fort Duquesne, there accompanied him a son of Sir Peter Halket, who was also Sir Peter Halket, acting at this time as aide-de-camp to Gen. Forbes, a major of the 42nd regiment. His mission on this occasion to America was principally to ascertain more definitely the fate of his father. In company with other officers of the Highland regiment and a company of Pennsylvania rifles, under Captain West and a few Indians from the neighborhood who had fought with the French on that fatal day, they proceeded to the scene of the conflict. One of the Indian guides had seen Sir Peter fall and had also witnessed the sad fate of the son and had no difficulty in identifying the spot. The thick-fallen leaves were removed and the two ghastly skeletons of father and son discovered as they had fallen. Upon examination, young Halket identified the remains of his father by a peculiar artificial tooth and exclaimed "it is my father' and sank into the arms of his scarce less affected companions. The two remains were wrapped in a Highland plaid and interred in a common grave and a volley was fired over their resting places. A stone was placed to mark the sacred spot and the little company marched silently and sadly away. For more than a century that stone remained to indicate to the visitor of this historic ground the last resting place of one of England's bravest soldiers and Scotland's noblest sons

Fort Cumberland Continued.

After the retirement of the troops under Col. Dunbar from Fort Cumberland a garrison was still maintained at that post for the protection of the frontier settlers. Col. James Innes held command there until in May, 1756, when he placed the command with Major James Livingston. Col. Adam Stephens succeeded Major Livingston in the fall of 1756. About the 1st of February, 1757, Washington, then commander-in-chief of the Virginia forces, established his headquarters at Fort Cumberland, where he remained until the middle of April, when Capt. Dagworthy was placed in command.

Marauding parties of Indians and French continued to harass the frontier, penetrating far eastward of Fort Cum-

Braddock's Watch

berland, murdering, scalping and plundering even in sight of the walls of the fort. Sieur Langlade, at the head of a detachment of French and Indians, advanced as far as Fort Cumberland in August, 1756, to ascertain the movements of the English, and after reconnoitering the locality retired without doing serious damage. Sieur de Celeron de Blainville, with a scouting party, encountered some English near the fort in August. Three of the English were killed and scalped; de Blainville and three Indians were killed. A detachment under de Celeron penetrated as far as Cressap's post, some 15 miles east of Fort Cumberland, and killed eight English.

About the middle of July, 1765, the last British troops were withdrawn from Fort Cumberland, and the frontier settlers were left to their own resources. This state of affairs, happily, was of short duration, as a treaty of peace between the whites and Indians was effected early in 1776.

When what is known as the "Whiskey Insurrection" took place in Western Pennsylvania in 1794, the President ordered out some government troops for its suppression. Some of the troops were quartered for a short time at Fort Cumberland. While here they were inspected by General Washington on the 19th of October, with Generals Lee and Morgan, General Washington appearing in full uniform. This is the last body of troops that ever occupied Fort Cumberland, and is said to be the last time in which Washington appeared in full uniform.

The stone structure, known as the Emmanuel Episcopal church, now occuipes a portion of the site of old Fort Cumberland.

General Washington, on his visit to the west in 1784, sought to visit the last resting place of his former commander, through respect for the same, but his search was in vain. He wrote: "I made diligent search for the grave, but the road had been so much turned and the clear land so much extended that it could not be found."

Mr. Abraham Stewart, father of the Hon. Andrew Stewart, was road supervisor, and in 1804, while repairing the Braddock road at this place, found human bones a few yards from the road.

BRADDOCK'S EXPEDITIONS 101

The military trappings found with them indicated that the remains were those of a British officer of rank, and as General Braddock was known to have been buried at this camp the bones doubtless were his. These bones were carefully gathered up and reinterred at a distance of one hundred and fifty yards eastward from the place they were found, at the foot of an oak tree. Mr. Stewart caused a board to be marked "Braddock's Grave," which was nailed to the tree. This tree was broken off during a severe storm about 1868. Mr. Josiah King, editor of the Pittsburgh Gazette, frequently spent a few weeks' vacation at Chalk Hill, in the vicinity of the grave of General Braddock, and noticing the dilapidated condition of this historic spot, made arrangements to have it enclosed by a neat and substantial fence. In 1872 he procured from Murdock's nursery a willow whose parent stem drooped over the grave of the Emperor Napoleon at St. Helena and planted it over the remains of General Braddock, but unfortunately it soon withered and died. He then planted a number of pine trees within the enclosure, which still remain to indicate to the passerby the last resting place of Major General Edward Braddock.

The British government has never taken the slightest notice of the spot where sleep the remains of one who gave his service and his life for the English cause. The situation is on the north side and a few yards from the national road, and a few rods east of where Braddock's run crosses that road, and about ten miles east of Uniontown.

"Far from the land he called his own,
  Nor friends nor kindred o'er him weep;
A group of forest trees alone,
  Stand sentinels around his sleep."

General Braddock's Watch.

The gold watch-case of which the above is an ilustration was found near the route of Braddock's retreating army in 1880, near a fine spring.

The case is a fine specimen of the engraver's skill and illustrates the legend of "The Judgment of Paris." Paris is represented in a sitting posture; with his right hand he is presenting the golden apple to Venus who stands before him. Beneath his feet are the figures of a dog and a quiver of arrows. Between Paris and Venus is the figure of Cupid. In the rear of Venus are the figures of Hera and Athens, the rivals of Venus. The owl, the helmet, the Shield and two peafowls are also represented.

It bears the name of the engraver, George Michael Moser, who excelled in his profession and flourished in the time of Braddock.

The dying general was carried along with the retreating army and doubtless this watch dropped from his pocket and was picked up by one of the frightened soldiers and hidden near a spring expecting some day to recover it, but the opportunity never came.

The works of the watch were corroded away when found and the case is now kept as a relic of that ill-fated expedition.

On July 4th, 1908, a tablet was erected to mark the grave of General Braddock containing the following inscription:

Here lie the mortal remains of
Major General Braddock,

who in command of the Forty-fourth and Forty-eighth regiments of English regulars, was mortally wounded in an engagement with the French and Indians under the command of de Beaujeu at the battle of the Monongahela, within ten miles of Fort Duquesne, July 9, 1755.

He was borne back with the retreating army to the Old Orchard camp, where he died July 13, 1755.

Erected July 4, 1908, under the auspices of the Centennial Celebration committee of 1904.

The Site of Braddock's Grave to be Made a Park.

In 1909, a number of spirited citizens of Uniontown, Pa., organized an association to be known as "The General Edward Braddock Memorial Park Association." The officers chosen were Edgar S. Hackney, cashier of the First National Bank, president; James Hadden, secretary and treasurer; and Edgar S. Hackney, James Hadden, W. C. McCormick, Chas. S. Seaton, Isaac W. Semans, E. H. Reppert, J. C. Work, W. A. Stone, and William Hunt, directors.

Braddock's Grave

Twenty-four acres of land, including the grave, have been secured by the association with the purpose of embellishing and preserving this historic spot.

CHAPTER III.

A Sketch of Thos. Fausett, the Slayer of Major General Edward Braddock, who Became a Resident of Fayette County, Pa.

The English Attempt to Drive the French from the Ohio Valley.

"Circumstances make strange bedfellows," and it was under peculiar circumstances that the name of Tom Fausett has become inseparably connected with that of the brave officer of the famous Cold Stream Guards, Major General Edward Braddock.

When France began the erection of a cordon of posts along the Allegheny and Ohio rivers with the purpose of taking possession of the great Mississippi valley, England was aroused to the fact that unless active measures be immediately taken she must forfeit all her claims to this vast and fertile portion of the new world.

English traders had been driven from their trading posts on the Ohio and others had been carried away as prisoners by the French, when Robert Dinwiddie, then governor of the province of Virginia, commissioned George Washington, then just twenty-one years of age, as an envoy to the French posts at the head of the Allegheny river to demand of the commandant of the French forces the purpose of their encroachment upon the territory claimed by the English crown, and to demand his immediate removal.

Being appraised of the intentions of the French, the governor of Virginia immediately dispatched a small force under the command of Captain Trent, Lieutenant Frasher and Ensign Ward, to take possession of the forks of the Ohio, and to hold the same against the intrusion of the French.

Ward began the construction of a small fort, but before its completion the French dropped down the Allegheny in great numbers and Ward, who was the only officer present at the time, was compelled to surrender without a blow, and retraced his steps to Virginia, and the French began the construction of a fort which they named Fort Duquesne.

At Will's creek, where the city of Cumberland now stands, Ward was met by Washington, who, in command of a small force, was on his way to the forks with reinforcements.

Washington Fights His First Battle and Defeats the French.

On reaching the Great Meadows, fifty-one miles west of Will's creek, Washington learned that a body of French had been seen not a great distance off, and by the aid of a few friendly Indians under the command of their chief, the Half-King, who were encamped at the Great Rock on the crest of Laurel Hill, he was enabled to surprise them in their secluded encampment. Here an engagement took place at sunrise on the morning of the 28th of May, 1754, in which Jumonville, the commander of the French party, and nine others were killed, one wounded and twenty-one taken prisoners, among whom were M. La

BRADDOCK'S EXPEDITIONS 109

Force, M. Drouillion and two cadets; one, a Canadian, escaped.

This was the first battle in which Washington was ever engaged, and was the initial battle of the great French and Indian war.

When the news of the defeat of Jumonville reached Fort Duquesne great activity prevailed and a force was sent against Washington under the command of M. Coulon de Villiers, who was a half-brother to Jumonville. This force came up the Monongahela river in large canoes to the mouth of Redstone creek, thence passing the place of the engagement with Jumonville to the Gerat Meadows, to which place Washington had retreated and erected a small stockade which he named Fort Necessity. Here on the third day of July, 1754, the French forces made an attack, and owning to the distressed condition of his little army, Washington capitulated; this being the first as well as the last time Washington ever surrendered to a foe.

News of this defeat was soon heralded to England and preparations were immediately made to send two regiments of trained soldiers to recover what the provincial troops had failed to accomplish.

General Braddock Lands in America.

Major General Edward Braddock had entered the British army at the age of fifteen years as a member of the Cold Stream Guards, a very aristocratic division of the army. He was commissioned general-in-chief of His Majesty's forces in North America and arrived at Alexandria in Virginia, February 20, 1755. Two regiments of the royal army, consisting of the Forty-fourth and Forty-eighth, to which were added such provincials as might be recrutied from Maryland and Virginia were moved against the French at the Forks of the Ohio, where they had erected Fort Duquesne immediately after the surrender of Ward as before mentioned, and thence to Canada.

After a long, tedious and laborious march, consuming more than a month from the time he left Fort Cumberland, General Braddock arrived at the Monongahela river, a short distance below the present town of McKeesport. The army crossed to the left bank of the river; here the maneuvers of the troops presented the grandest military display Washington claimed it was ever his privilege to behold. The burnished arms of the marching columns flashed in the light of the morning sun as they stepped to the strains of martial music, and the proud British general little thought that within a few short hours these disciplined troops in which he now reposed so much confidence would be fleeing in disorder before a horde of yelling savages.

The army had scarcely recrossed to the right bank of the river, just below the mouth of Turtle creek, and within ten miles of the fort which they expected to enter in triumph the following day, when a brisk fire was received from an unseen foe. Braddock's troops responded, but to little effect and the engagement which lasted for three hours was most furious.

Braddock Meets a Disastrous Defeat.

More than half of the army was either killed or wounded, two-thirds of them being shot down by their own men. Braddock had four horses killed under him; at last, while on the fifth, he received a mortal wound which shattered his right arm and penetrated his lungs. He was wrapped in a silken sash taken from about his waist, which English officers were wont to carry, and by his aids, Captain Orme and Captain Stewart of Virginia, assisted by his faithful body servant, Bishop, whom in his dying moments he bequeathed to Washington, he was carried off the field. This silken sash was later presented to General Zachary Taylor and contains woven in its meshes the initials "E. B." and is marked with blood stains of that unfortunate general. It was in the possession of Mrs. Bettie Dandridge, the daughter of President Taylor, of Winchester, Va., until her death.

Out of eighty-nine commissioned officers twenty-six were killed and thirty-seven wounded, and of the soldiers four hundred and thirty were killed and about four hundred wounded, the killed being in excess of the wounded. Every field officer and every one on horseback except Washington, who had two horses

BRADDOCK'S EXPEDITIONS 113

killed under him and four bullets through his coat, was either killed or carried off the field wounded. Washington, although enfeebled and emaciated from fever, formed and covered the retreat.

The officers endeavored in vain to rally the distracted troops, and to intimidate others ran the fugitives through with the sword, and were in turn killed by others. One eye witness declared that the slaughter among the officers was not made by the enemy, but as they had run several fugitives through the body to intimidate the rest, when they were attempting in vain to rally them, some others who expected the same fate fired their pieces with deadly effect.

During the whole of the engagement Braddock raved and swore and cursed his troops as dastards and cowards. The provincials, being acquainted with the Indian mode of warfare, had taken to the trees and were doing good execution, but Braddock ordered them to stand out, as he said, "like English soldiers" and fight in the open. He struck many of them down with his sword, among whom was Joseph Fausett, a brother to the subject of this sketch, and for which act he paid the penalty with his life.

Braddock was described as "desperate in his fortune, brutal in his behavior and obstinate in his sentiments." His secretary writes of him before the battle "We have a general most judiciously chosen for being disqualified for the service in which he is employed in almost every respect."

Tom Fausett Fires the Fatal Shot.

Thomas Fausett and his brother, Joseph Fausett, were enlisted as privates at six pence a day, at Shippensburg, Pennsylvania, by Captain William Polson, who had served under Washington in the expedition of 1754, into Captain Cholmondeley's company of the 48th regiment, and marched with the advance of Braddock's army to the fatal field.

During the engagement Tom witnessed the fearful slaughter of the army by the unseen foe, the raving madness of his commander and the striking down of his brother for no other offense than that of fighting in the only successful manner against the Indians. This was too much for a man of his temperament to stand and he determined at once to have revenge and at the same time to put an end to the terrible carnage for which the officers had pleaded in vain. He raised his gun and sent the deadly missile crashing through the right arm and into the lungs of Braddock, who as he fell from his horse expressed the wish that the scene of his defeat might witness his death.

While this rash act of Fausett can never be palliated but deserves hearty condemnation, the affection he had for his brother, the love he bore toward his comrades and countrymen and his admiration for Washington appealed to his untutored mind and brutal instinct more forcibly than his loyalty to his commander.

The wounded commander was borne along with the retreating army until 10 o'clock of the evening of the following day, when they arrived at Gist's plantation, in the exact geographical center of what is now Fayette county. Here he awaited provisions and hospital stores which he had ordered sent forward from Col. Dunbar, who was encamped on the summit of Laurel Hill, six miles distant. Braddock still persisted in the exercise of his authority, and on the 11th was removed to Dunbar's camp which he found to be in the utmost confusion. Here he ordered the provisions and ammunition destroyed lest they fall into the hands of the enemy. One hundred and fifty wagons were burned, the powder casks were staved and their contents, to the amount of 50,000 pounds, cast into the stream. Nothing beyond the actual necessities of a flying march was saved, and until recent years this has been a fruitful field for the relic seekers.

Gen. Braddock Dies, and Tom Fausett Locates the Grave 57 Years Afterward.

On Sunday, the 13th, the army retraced its steps to the Old Orchard camp where it had halted on its way out. The general softly repeated to himself: "Who would have thought it?" and turning to Orme said, "We shall better know how to deal with them another time." He breathed his last about 8 o'clock on the same night and was wrapped in his cloak as a winding sheet and was buried at daybreak on Monday morning at the camp in the middle of the road that the army in passing over the grave might obliterate every trace of its whereabouts, and thus avoid any desecration of the body by the Indians. The chaplain having been wounded, Washington read the Episcopal funeral service and the dead general was buried in the honors of war.

Abraham Stewart, father of the late Honorable Andrew Stewart, was road supervisor in Wharton township in 1804, and while repairing the old road at this place Tom Fausett, who had settled in this neighborhood after the retreat of the army, as will be related hereafter, came along where the men were at work and remarked, "If you will dig right there," indicating, "you will find the bones of General Braddock," and sure enough, Mr. Stewart dug as directed and exhumed the bones of the unfortunate general and his military trappings. A merchant happened to witness the discovery and carried off one of the largest bones which he placed in Peale's museum in Philadelphia where it was destroyed by fire. Mr. Stewart carefully reinterred the remainder of the bones at a distance of one hundred and fifty yards east of the place where they were found, at the foot of an oak tree and caused a board to be marked "Braddock's Grave," which was nailed to a tree. This tree was broken off in a severe storm about 1868. Mr. James Mitchell, a blacksmith, who lived at Mt. Washington, and Mr. Peter Hager, who was raised in the family of Mr. Stewart, with others witnessed the reinterment of Braddock's remains and often related the circumstances to others.

Mr. Josiah King, editor of the Pittsburg Gazette, frequently spent a few weeks' vacation at Chalk Hill in the vicinity of the grave of General Braddock, and noticing the dilapidated condition of this historic spot, made arrangements with Mr. Dixon, the proprietor of the land, to have it enclosed with a neat and substantial fence. In 1872, he procured from Murdock's nursery a willow whose parent stem drooped over the grave of the Emperor Napoleon at St. Helena and planted it over the remains of General Braddock, but unfortunately it soon withered and died. He then planted a number of pine trees within the enclosure which still remain to indicate to passers by the last resting place of the unfortunate general.

The British government has never taken the slightest notice of the spot where sleep the remains of one who gave his service and his life for the English cause.

"Far from the land he called his own,
  Nor friends nor kindred o'er him weep;
A group of forest trees alone
  Stand sentinels around his sleep."

The situation is on the north side and a few yards from the national road and a few rods east of where Braddock's run crosses that road, about ten miles east of Uniontown.

Tom Fausett, the slayer of Braddock, was a large illiterate, muscular man of great strength, rude habits and strong passions. His brother, Joseph, was doubtless the same, and, as before stated, both were enlisted and served in the same company during the expedition.

When Braddock's retreating army passed over the mountains confusion prevailed and many deserted from the ranks, among whom were Tom and Joe Fausett.

Washington's Springs on the Crest of Laurel Hill Once Owned by Tom Fausett.

The next we learn of Tom Fausett we find him located on the summit of Laurel Hill at the junction of Dunlap's road, which led to the Monongahela river at the mouth of Dunlap's creek, with the Braddock road, which here turned abruptly to the north and on to Gist's and to Stewart's crossing of the Youghiogheny river a short distance below the present town of Connellsville.

This location has always been known as Washington's Springs and was on a tract of 102¾ acres of land which was warranted the 17th of September, 1772, to Henry Hunt. Here Fausett conducted a tavern for some years, besides spending much of his time in hunting the wild game so abundant in those days. A writer in the National Intelligencer, supposed to have been the late William Darby, Esy., said: "When my father was removing with his family to the west one of the Fausetts kept a public house eastward from Uniontown, with whom we lodged about the 10th of Oc-

Washington's Springs

tober, 1781, and there it was made anything but a secret that he dealt the death blow to the British general. Thirteen years afterwards, 1794, I again met Tom Fausett and put to him the plain question, 'Did you shoot General Braddock?' and his reply was prompt and explicit, 'I did shoot him,' and then went on to explain that by so doing he had contributed to save what was left of the army.

The property rolls of Wharton township give Tom Fausett as located here and having in his possession horses and cows as taxables. How Fausett acquired the right to this tract is not apparent, but on April 29th, 1788, he disposed of it as the following abstract from the public records will show:

"Know all men by these present that I, Thomas Fossit, of the county of Phayette and state of Pennsylvania for and in Consideration of the sum of Fifty Pounds to Mee In hand Paid by Isaac Philips of the same Place the Receipt whereof I do acknowledge have Granted, bargained, sold, Releas'd, confirmed and made over all My rite tract of Land and Parcel of Land I now live Upon at the forks of the Road on the top of Laurel Hill Known by the name of Washington's Spring adjoining the Lands of Jonathan Hill Els whereby Vacant Land Containing one hundred acres More or less To Have and to Hold the said tract of Land and premises and appertenances thereunto belonging unto the said Isaac Phillips his heirs Heirs and assigns warranting and defending it all, Every of My self My heirs or any Claim or Claiming by virtue of My Rite and title to said Land only nevertheless under and Subject to the States and it all other dues and Demands unto which the same are Liable.

In witness whereof I Have set my Hand and seal hereunto. Dated the 29th day of April in the year of our Lord one Thousand Seven Hundred Eighty Eight.

his
THOMAS X FOSSET, seal"
mark.

A few years after Fausett had disposed of his claim to the Washington's Springs tract it came into the possession of John Slack who had previously kept a tavern in Uniontown. Slack's tavern stood some little distance south of the Washington's Springs and here he conducted his business for many years. This was a favorite stopping place and was extensively known and patronized by the wagoners on the old road. His daughter, Tamzon, married Ephraim McClean who kept a public house on the summit of Laurel Hill in the palmy days of the old national road. Slack's place was considered a good stand for the entertainment of the traveling public until the completion of the national road, at which time the old Braddock road was abandoned and quiet once more settled over the old Nemacolin trail.

Tom Fausett was said to have been married three times and that two of his wives were killed by the Indians, and that his favorite, as he termed her his "little Dutch wife," was tomahawked before his eyes. There is no tradition in this section of the country that he had a wife after settling here, but after retiring from the tavern business and disposing of his tract of land he remained a citizen of Wharton township, and for some time occupied a cabin on the old Braddock road back of Chalk Hill. This old cabin was west of what was long known as the Cushman house, the location of which is still visible, and still west of his old cabin is a group of immense rocks known as the "Peddler's Rocks." With this picturesque group of rocks is connected the legend that at one time a peddler was murdered here for his money and pack of jewelry and other valuables which he carried. His pack and other articles were found secreted among these rocks, but what became of the peddler was never certainly known, but suspicion rested upon more than one of the several persons living in the neighborhood of the rocks.

While Tom Fausett occupied this old cabin, making a precarious living with his gun, he had as his housekeeper an old colored woman who had been a slave. One morning upon calling his housekeeper and receiving no response he went to her couch and found her cold in death. She was buried in a field some distance away between two apple trees, as markers, and as there was no minister present to conduct the funeral service one of the neighbors deeming it appropriate

Peddler's Rocks

that some remarks should be made at the grave, ventured the following:

"Earth to earth and dust to dust,
If the Lord wont take her the devil must."

Joseph Fausett, although struck down with the sword of the enraged Braddock, survived, and also became a resident of Wharton township, and left descendants. One of his sons, Joseph Fausett, Jr., married Amelia Lynch, daughter of Cornelius Lynch of Uniontown, who at one time owned and occupied the ground now covered by the Thompson-Ruby building, corner Main and Morgantown streets. This son, Joseph, owned a farm north of Chalk Hill and died young, leaving a wife and two small children, Joseph and Elizabeth, the latter of whom is well remembered by the older citizens of Uniontown. The widow, as administratrix, sold the farm, September 28th, 1800, to John Chaplin who in turn conveyed the same to Jonathan Downer. Another son of the original Joseph Fausett was Uriah who left quite a family of which one daughter, Rebecca, made her home in Wharton township until old age overtook her when she was sent to the county home, to which institution she was admitted May 17, 1906, and where she died Jan. 9, 1910, aged 84 years, having made her home for more than forty years with William Smith and was later the housekeeper of Isaac Spiker a short distance east of Farmington.

Tom Fausett Confesses That He Fired the Fatal Shot That Killed Braddock.

Tom Fausett never denied that he fired the shot that killed Braddock, but upon repeated occasions, especially when in his cups, did he relate the circumstances which prompted him to commit the deed. Besides the confessions already recited, Mr. Freeman Lewis, who assisted Judge Veech in collecting data in compiling his "Monongahela of Old," recites that he at one time taught a country school and one day when the children were at play he heard the cry of "There's old Tom Fausett, the man who killed Braddock." The children feared him, his appearance and noisiness, especially when intoxicated, being rather terrifying. I knew him and got him to sit down by a tree. He at once began fluttering his fingers over his mouth to imitate the roll of a drum, he soon got at his old rigmarole, which ran about thus: Poor fellows—poor fellows—they are all gone—murdered by a madman—Braddock was a madman—he would not let us tree, but made us stand out and be shot down when we could see no Indians;—Yes, Braddock was a madman. He said, "No skulking, no treeing, but stand out and give them fair English play." If he had been shot when the battle began and Washington had taken command we would have licked them,—yes, we'd a licked then." "How could you have done that?" I asked. "Why, we'd 'ave charged on them, and driven them out of the brush and peavines,—then we would have seen their red skins and could have peppered them—yes, we'd have peppered their red skins." He would then repeat his "boo-oo-oo my old Virginia Blues—poor fellows—all gone," &c., &c., and tears would roll over his rough cheeks.

Fausett often related the circumstances of the killing of Braddock to the late Hon. Andrew Stewart, who served eighteen years in congress, who when a young man and a resident of Wharton township was intimately acquainted with Fausett, then in his old age. Peter Hager, who was raised as a member of the family of Abraham Stewart, and who assisted in removing the bones of General Braddock, repeatedly heard Fausett relate the circumstances of the killing of what he termed the madman.

The late Basil Brownfield of South Union township, who was born near the present site of Smithfield, related that Tom Fausett frequently visited that locality on huting expeditions, and that by frequent interviews with him he learned that the Fausetts were at one time residents of the South Branch valley, in the present state of West Virginia, from the neighborhood of the site of Moorefield, and that Tom's principal occupation was that of a hunter.

One time on returning from a huting expedition he was horrified at finding his cabin in ashes and the dead and scalped bodies of his wife and children a short distance off where they had been overtaken and slaughtered by the Indians. He could never refer to this incident without manifesting great emotion and tears would roll down his rugged cheeks. He said he could not remain in the vicinity where his family had been killed, and removed to Pennsylvania where he and his brother enlisted in Braddock's campaign.

Mr. Brownfield further related that Fausett was a man of rugged frame, of uninviting features, distant in his manners, rarely associating with others, was not communicative when sober but inclined to be boisterous and boastful when intoxicated. He frequently related to Mr. Brownfield that he fired the fatal shot at Braddock in revenge for striking his brother and for other offenses.

It is related that an Indian trader by the name of McCullough used to travel an Indian trail leading from Winchester to the west and the trail became known as McCullough's path. This McCullough was in the habit of supplying the Indians, even in times of war, with knives, hatchets, powder and balls. The settlers threatened him for this but he would not desist. Learning when he was to pass that way a number of settlers disguised themselves and went in pursuit. They caught and threatened him with dire punishment unless he gave up his nefarious traffic. He at first refused to comply with their wishes, but Tom Fausett, being one of the party, caught McCullough in his giant grasp and held him until his tormentors made him promise never more to transgress, and after despoiling him of his peltry, they let him go, and he never was seen again in that region of country.

Writers upon this unfortunate expedition are wont to cast a doubt as to the manner in which Braddock received his death wound, and produce conflicting rumors to dispute the statements made by Fausett. No one who was acquainted with Fausett, knew his disposition and habits, doubted his statement as to the death of the British general. Freeman Lewis, previously referred to, stated that his last interview with Fausett was in the month of October, 1816, and that Fausett then claimed to be one hundred and four years of age, and that his appearance bore him out, and that some of Fausett's statements were "wholly irreconcilable with well ascertained facts." Who would expect an illiterate man at

Rebecca Fausett
Grand-daughter of Joseph Fausett

that extreme age to relate circumstances in detail with perfect accuracy that had transpired a half century before?

Winthrop Sargent in his "Braddock's Expedition" goes some length to disprove the statements made by Faucett, while at the same time he adduces the evidence of William Butler who had served as a private in the Pennsylvania Greens at the defeat of Braddock, and under Forbes in 1758, and under Wolf in 1759, at the Plains of Abraham, who when interrogated as to the killing of Braddock unhesitatingly declared that he was shot by Fausett for striking down his brother. The Millerstown (Perry county, Pa.) Gazette of 1830, mentions the fact that Butler was in that town in company with another who had served under Braddock and that both concurred in saying that Braddock had been killed by Fausett.

The Colonization Herald (Philadelphia) of June 20. 1838, contained the notice of the death of William Butler at the age of one hundred and eight years, and further states that he had lived at the corner of Sixth and Chestnut streets, which was then in woods and leaning on his crutch, often entertained visitors by a recital of the unfortunate expedition and the circumstances of the death of Braddock.

The evidence of Billy Brown, a negro living at Frankfort, Pennsylvania, taken in 1826, when he was ninety-three years of age is also adduced to confirm Fausett's story. He was born in Africa and brought as a slave to this country at an early age. He was present at Braddock's defeat as a servant to a colonel in the Irish regiment. He relates that Braddock's character was obstinate and profane and he also confirms the report that Braddock was shot **by an American** because he had killed, or was supposed to have killed, his brother, and that none seemed to care for it.

Daniel Adams of Newberryport, Massachusetts, states that in 1842, it had been told him by one who had it from another who was present at the occurrence that the principal officers had desired a retreat which the general pertinaciously refused and upon seeing the rashness of the commander a brother of one who had been stricken down fired the fatal shot, which several of the soldiers witnessed but said nothing.

Historian Sargent in his effort to disprove that Braddock met his death at the hands of Fausett not only admits but certainly establishes the fact that such was the current belief at the time among those in position to know.

A still further witness who heretofore has entirely escaped the notice of the historian is James Edwards, who was a captain in one of the Associated Companies of Kent county, now Delaware, in August, 1748, in the service of the Province of Pennsylvania. He enlisted in Braddock's campaign, and in the defeat was wounded in the leg by a musket ball, which he carried to his grave. He subsequently served in the Revolutionary war in Colonel Thomas Proctor's celebrated artillery in preference to infantry on account of his wounded leg, and served at Brandywine, Chadd's Ford, Newtown, Germantown, Bergen Neck and Trenton. Mr. Edwards finally settled at Barnegat, New Jersey, where he was a prominent member of the Methodist Episcopal church. He too lived to an advanced age and frequently related the scenes of

Braddock's defeat and always positively asserted that the unfortunate general was killed by one of his own men by the name of Fausett for striking down his brother and, as he thought, uselessly sacrificing the lives of his soldiers. Mr. Edwards was an ardent admirer of Washington and in his old age expressed his willingness to depart and join his "dear old General, Washington," whom he believed to be "one of the brightest stars in the region of glory." Mr. Edwards is buried in the Methodist church yard at Tuckerton, New Jersey.

It will be remembered that Braddock's army precipitately fled from the fatal field and scattered like leaves before the hurricane, but Sargent does not account for the fact that William Butler, of Philadelphia, and Billy Brown of Frankfort, Pennsylvania and Daniel Adams of Newberryport, Massachusetts, and James Edwards of New Jersey, and many others, having no communication whatever with each other all concurred in relating substantially the same story as Fausett unless they had gotten these facts before the army was disbanded at Fort Cumberland on the retreat.

The evidence here adduced is certainly all that would be necessary to warrant conviction in a court of justice were Fausett on trial for firing the fatal shot at the British general.

Tom Fausett Becomes a Charge Upon the Township of Wharton.

For some years before his death Tom Fausett became a charge upon the township of Wharton, and it was the custom to sell out paupers to the lowest bidder. In an old book still extant, kept by the overseers of the poor for that township, are the following entries:

"March 20, 1812, Be it remembered that James Wear has undertaken to keep Thomas Fausett for the space of one year for the sum of thirty-seven dollars and seventy-five cents exclusive of finding him any clothing.

March 19, 1813, Samuel Spaugh undertakes to keep Thomas Fausett one year for the sum of thirty-seven dollars and seventy-five cents, exclusive of finding him any clothing.

April 4, 1814, For the keeping of Fausett for one year, fifty-seven dollars. For selling Fausett in 1814, $1.00.

For the keeping of Fausett for the year 1815, $39.80.

March 15, 1816, Be it remembered that Thomas Mitchell undertakes to keep Thomas Fausett, one of the poor of Wharton township, for one year for forty-eight dollars, exclusive of finding him clothing.

March 21, 1817, Be it remembered that Edward Tissue undertakes to keep Thomas Fausett, one of the poor of Wharton township, exclusive of finding him clothing, for one year for $37.50.

March 20, 1818, Be it remembered that Thomas Mitchell undertakes to keep Thomas Fausett, one of the poor of Wharton township, exclusive of finding him clothing for twenty-eight dollars and fifty cents, the time not to commence until the 24th of April.

April 24, 1819, Be it remembered that Thomas Mitchell undertakes to board, lodge and wash and mend and find tobacco for Thomas Fausett for one year from this date for the sum of fifty dollars.

Auditors' report for 1819. By noticing the sale of Fausett for the present year,

50 cents, tobacco for Fausett, 25 cents, paid for keeping Fausett twenty-eight dollars and fifty cents.

April 24, 1819. By one day selling Faucett and settling with auditors, $1.00.

1820, Contra. Moses Mercer and John Bolin, overseers of the poor, Cr. by keeping Thomas Fausett, fifty dollars.

By Fausett clothing and Mercer, his attendance, sixty-two dollars and seventy-five cents."

From this last entry it would appear that poor old Tom had been deprived of clothing until he had no further use of the same. Then the township furnished a suit in order that he might appear the more respectable in the happy hunting grounds.

This last entry in this old township book would indicate that Tom Fausett died in 1820, and that Moses Mercer was in attendance at his death and burial, and that the overseers of the poor settled the bill of expenses. From the fact that Faucett's name does not again appear on the book the inference would be reasonable that he died during the year 1820.

For some years before his death Fausett made his home in a little log cabin which stood on what was subsequently the Frederick Nicolay farm about one mile and a half west of Ohiopyle Falls. Here he cultivated among other things a little patch of tobacco for his own use which he husbanded with the greatest care. This old cabin, like its tenant, has long since passed away, but after nearly a half century had rolled away since the death of its distinguished occupant, Mr. Nicolay was plowing near the site of the old cabin, a few stones of the old chimney only remaining, near which his plow turned up a small box containing a quantity of silver coins and jewelry. He took his find to Pittsburgh for the purpose of ascertaining its value, the coins being in different denominations of foreign money such as was current in those early days, and placed it in charge of an old acquaintance and well known banker of that city, but nothwithstanding his frequent inquiries he died before he ascertained the value or recovered his valuable discovery.

The finding of this box of jewelry and coin revived the story that was current in the mountain region of Wharton township many years before, as pre-

Grave of Thomas Fausett

BRADDOCK'S EXPEDITIONS

viously related, that a peddler had been murdered at the Peddlers Rocks near the cabin of Fausett, and the discovery of this box with its peculiar contents would indicate that Fausett might have known somewhat of the missing peddler.

Fausett's last home was in the family of Thomas Mitchell, about two miles west of Ohiopyle Falls. He was buried in a small burying ground on what was known as the Jacob H. Rush farm, since occupied by the late Patton Rush, where also rest the remains of many of the old residents of that neighborhood. Some years after his death a rude headstone was erected to his memory on which is inscribed the following:

THO FAUCET
died
March 23
1822
Aged 109
9 mos

Thus is marked the last resting place of the slayer of Major General Edward Braddock, and on each recurring memorial day a flag and a few flowers are placed on the little mound of earth to keep his memory green.

INDEX

----, Bishop 82 87 112
    Black Hunter The
    71 Black Rifle The
    71 Capt Jack 70-72
    Susquehanna Jack
    71 Wild Hunter of
    The Juniata 71
ACKERMANN, Karen
    13
ADAMS, Daniel 132
    134
AMIABLE, Charlotte
    26
ARMSTRONG, Col 47
B, E 112
BEAZELL, John W 65
BEESON, A G 63
    Isaac 47 58-59
BIERER, Everhart 63
BOLIN, John 137
BONAPARTE,
    Napoleon 101 118
BOWMAN, M H 64
BOYLE, T N 65
BRADDOCK, 11 38-42
    45-48 50 70-72 74-
    75 78-79 81 84-87
    89-90 94-95 111-
    116 119 125-127
    129-134 Edward 67
    102 106 110 139
    Gen 68-69 76 88

BRADDOC (continued)
    101 103-104 110
    117-118 121 128
    Maj Gen 67 69 103
BRODDOCK, Edward
    67
BROOKS, William 55-
    56
BROWN, Billy 132 134
    Wendell 12
BROWNFIELD, Basil
    128 Mr 129
BRYSON, Samuel 43
BURGOYNE, 69
BURTON, Col 93 Lt
    Col 70
BUTLER, William 131
    134
CABOT, 7
CAMPBELL, Samuel
    Y 58-59
CARSON, Hampton L
    65
CHAPLIN, John 125
CHAPMAN, Maj 70
    75-76 85
CHOLMONDELEY,
    Capt 88 114
CLARK, 54 James 70
CLARKE, F 60
COBURN, Camden M
    65

CONNELLY, Dr 37
CONTRECOEUR, 17-18 20 28
CONTRECOUR, M De 84
CRAIK, Dr 43 76
    George Washington 43
    James 42
CRESAP, Thomas 10
CRESSAP, 99
CROGHAN, George 16 45 70
CROMWELL, Violet 46 William 46
CRUMRINE, Boyd 65
CUMBERLAND, Duke of 69
CURRAM, 13
CUSHMAN, 124
DAGWORTHY, Capt 38 98
DANDRIDGE, Bettie 112 Betty 82
DARBY, William 120
DAVIDSON, John 13 Thomas R 59
DAVIS, Mr 95 Owen 95
DAWSON, K 61
DEBEAUJEU, 84 104
DEBLAINVILLE, Sieur De Celeron 99
DECELERON, 99
DELAFIELD, Maj 60
DEVILLIERS, 35 51 M Coulon 34 37 66 109

DEYARMON, T Robb 62
DINWIDDIE, Gov 12 15 19 26 39-41 54 69 91 Robert 8 107
DIXON, Mr 118
DOLLIVER, J P 65
DOWNER, Jonathan 125
DROUILLION, 26 M 109
DUMAS, 84
DUNBAR, 83 86-88 116 Col 68 76 84-86 90 93-94 98 115 Thomas 69
DUNMORE, 42
EDMUNDSTONE, Charles 55
EDWARDS, James 133-134 Mr 133-134
ELS, Jonathan Hill 122
EVANS, Samuel 57
EWING, Nathaniel 57
FAUCET, Tho 139
FAUSETT, 115 122 127 131-134 139 Amelia 125 Eliz 125 Joe 119 Joseph 113-114 119 125 Joseph Jr 125 Rebecca 125 Thomas 114 135-137 Tom 106 117 119-121 123-124 126 128 130 135 137 Uriah 125

FAZENBAKER,
    Godfrey 57-58
    Lewis 58 Mr 57
FLENNIKEN, R P 59
    Robert P 58
FORBES, Gen 96-97
    John 95-96
FOSSET, Thomas 122
FOSSIT, Joseph 89
    Thomas 88 121
    Tom 89
FRANKLIN, Benjamin
    49 76
FRASHER, Lt 107
FRAZER, 13-15 91
    John 16 Lt 17
FRAZIER, 13
FRY, Col 28-29 42
    Joshua 19
GAGE, Col 80 Lt Col
    70 76 Thomas 80
GANS, John L 63
GATES, Capt 69
GILMORE, Saml A 59
GIST, 11-12 14-16 30-
    31 33-34 51 79 85
    115 120
    Christopher 9 13
    44 70 Mr 23 Nancy
    44 46 Nathaniel
    44-46 Richard 44
    46 Thomas 44-47
    Violet 44
GLADDEN, W H 65
GRANT, 38 Maj 41
HACKNEY, Edgar S
    104
HADDEN, James 64
    104

HAGER, Peter 118 128
HALKET, James 96
    Peter 68-69 75 83
    93 96-97
HALL, Chas 63
HAMBURG, John 8
HOPWOOD, Robert F
    64
HOWELL, Joshua B
    58-59
HUNT, Henry 120
    William 104
HUSTON, John 58
    Joseph 57
INDIAN, Half-king 9
    17 21-24 27 29 33
    49 51 70 73 78 108
    Manacatootha 74
    Monacatootha 13
    24 70 73
    Monacatooths 72-
    73 Nemacolin 10-
    11 Queen
    Aliquippa 29 43
    Scarooyada 24 50
    72 75 Serreneatta
    17 Tanacharission
    The Half-king 13
    Tanacharisson 9
    48 73
    Tannacharison The
    Half-king 28
INNES, Col 54 Gov 38
    James 37 54 98
JACK, Patrick 72
JENKINS, 13 Samuel
    95
JOHNS, Jay W 63
JONCAIRE, 14

JUMONVILLE, 28 33-
  34 36-37 39 41 48-
  49 51 78-79 86
  108-109 Monsieur
  25 N Coulon De 25
  27
KAINE, Daniel 58
KEENER, I E 64
KEIFER, M A 63
KENNEDY, Ralph C
  64
KEPPEL, Augustus 68
KING, Josiah 101 118
KNOX, P C 65
LAFORCE, 23 26 M
  108-109
LAMBING, A A 65
LANGDALE, Charles
  De 84
LANGLADE, Sieur 99
LEE, Gen 100 Thomas
  8
LEIS, Gen 42
LEMERCIER, 17
LESLIE, Matthew 70
LEWIS, Andrew 41
  Capt 30-31
  Freeman 126 130
LIVINGSTON, James
  98 Maj 98
LLOYD, F E J 64
LUDINGTON, M I 65
  Zalmon 58
LYNCH, Amelia 125
  Cornelius 125
MACKAYE, Capt 30-
  31 35 37 50 52 54
  66 Col 37 James 29
  36

MCCLEAN, Ephraim
  123 Tamzon 123
MCCORMICK, W C
  104
MCCULLOUGH, 129-
  130
MCQUIRE, 13
MEASON, Isaac 47-48
  Isaac Jr 47
  Thomas 57
MERCER, Dr 48 Hugh
  47-48 70 Moses
  137
MILHOLLAND, James
  A 55
MITCHELL, Ames 118
  Thomas 89 136 139
MONTOUR, 70
MORGAN, Gen 100
MORRIS, Harvey 58-
  59
MOSER, George
  Michael 103
MOUCEAU, 25
MURDOCK, 101 118
MUSE, Adjutant 40
  Maj 29
NICOLAY, Frederick
  138 Mr 138
ORME, Capt 82-83 94
  112 Robert 70
PARKMAN, Francis
  25
PARKS, Andrew 57
  Harriet 57
PATRICK, J N H 61
PERRY, 87
PEYRONIE, Ensign 42
PHILIPS, Isaac 121

PHILLIPS, Isaac 89
POLSON, Capt 30-31
   92 William 42 114
PROCTOR, Thos 133
REPPERT, E H 64 104
   Judge 64
RITENOUR, John S 65
RUSH, Jacob H 139
   Patton 139
   Sebastian 59
   Sebastion 58
RUTHEFORD, Capt 69
RUTHERFORD, 54
RUTTER, 63
SAINTPIERRE, 15 19
   Gen 12-13
   Legardeur De 14
SAMPEY, James 57 60
SARGENT, 133-134
   Winthrop 131
SEATON, Chas S 104
SEMANS, Isaac W 104
SHIRLEY, 83 Gov 86
   Maj Gen 38
SHREEVE, Israel 58
SINCLAIR, John 69-70 75 85 93 95
SLACK, John 122
   Tamzon 123
SLOAN, L S 63
SMITH, C W 65
   William 126
SPARKS, Maj 70
SPAUGH, Samuel 135
SPIKER, Isaac 126
STEPHENS, Adam 20 38 98 Gen 38
STEWART, 13 120
   Abraham 100 117 128 Andrew 58-59 62 100 117 127 Capt 82 112 David Shriver 61 Mr 60 101 117-118
STEWART (continued)
   Thomas 89-90
   William 22
STOBO, 40 Capt 32 41
   Robert 36 39
   William 39
STONE, W A 104
   William 58
STURGEON, Daniel 58
STURGIS, George C 65
TAYLOR, Bettie 112
   Betty 82 Pres 112
   Zachary 82 112
THOMAS, Lott 65
TISSUE, Edward 136
TRENT, 16 Capt 17 107 Wm 15
VANBRAAM, 39 41
   Jacob 13 36 40
VANSWEARINGEN, 37-38
VEECH, Judge 126
VILLIERS, Coulon 36
WAGGENER, Thomas 48
WARD, 28 108 110
   Edward 16 Ensign 16-20 49 107
WASHINGTON, 13-15 19-23 23-26 30 32-35 38-39 41-42

WASHINGTON
(continued)
44-45 48-54 57-58
70 76 78-80 82-83
85 87-88 91 98
108-109 111-115
117 127 134
Augustine 8 Col 18
Gen 55 100 Geo 94
George 8 12 36 40
55-56 66 107 John
58 Laurence 29
Lawrence 8 40 Maj
29 Maj Gen 27-28
Pres 43

WATERS, John A 64
WEAR, James 135
WEST, Capt 97 Lt 21
WHITE, F G 65
WOLF, 131 Gen 40
WORK, J C 104

www.ingramcontent.com/pod-product-compliance
Lightning Source LLC
Chambersburg PA
CBHW070922180426
43192CB00037B/1714